THE BAD BYTCH RULE BOOK

BY

JUICEY ADOIR

<u>MY DEDICATION</u>

This book is dedicated to all the real bytchez I know.

Pre-Face

"When trouble arises and things look bad, there is always one individual who perceives a solution and is willing to take command. Very often that individual is considered crazy." – Dave Berry

We live in a world where what looks like crazy is ordinary. Nothing ever really suprises me anymore. I learned never to put shyt past anyone. This world feels cold at times. Wondering who to trust and who not to. It's more fake bytchez out there then there are real ones. Everyone is starting to feel suspect. My circle is getting so small it's almost a dot at this point. So what do you do? Do you curl up in a little ball and go home? Or do fight for your respect and fight for your dreams?!? Do you have goals or are you just fighting for everyday survival?

I'm a realist. I been in a lot of different situations in a span of several years. I know and understand that there is a lot of women out there whom simply do not want better for themselves. They don't have the drive and determination to pursue better. The sad part is, these same women also don't want better for the people they see around them. Instead of focusing their time and energy on getting themselves together, they become bitter haters. This book right here is for any woman out there that has had run-ins with these hating ass bytchez.

This book will be your key to survival in this age in time. I represent for the women out there who have goals and are willing to work hard every day to make sure that their family is consistently moving forward.

They say the game is to be sold, and not to be told so I hope this copy your reading of this book was purchased and is yours to keep. **Write in it, Highlight in it, take notes. Carry this book with you and refer back to it whenever you need to. Prosperity is your birth right.** Begin to claim yours today!

I promise you this, there is a rule for each and every situation that you could ever find yourself into. This is the resource you need to build yourself a brighter future with what you have in hand today. You will have rules that are your favorites, you will have rules which you don't feel as much. Abide by the rules, or do not play the game.

"Civilization had too many rules for me, so I did my best to rewrite them." – Bill Cosby

CAUTION

"The Lord is my shepherd: I shall not want.
He maketh me to lie down in green pastures:
He leadeth me beside the still waters.
He restoreth my soul:
He leadeth me in the paths if righteousness for his
name's sake.
Yea, though I walk through the valley of the shadow of
death,
I will fear no evil: for thou art with me;
Thy rod and thy staff they comfort me.
Thou prepares a table before me in the presence of
mine enemies:
My cup runneth over.
Surely goodness and mercy shall follow me all the days
of my life:
And I will dwell in the house of the Lord forever."
-Psalms 23

The wrong mentality claims more lives of young adults then violence itself. It is up to you to provide yourself with the proper environment for your spirit to live in and grow. Would you plant a rosebush in the middle of the desert, where it would not receive the proper nutrition to live and grow?

This book will help you see past your daily circumstances and into your future. This book is not for the weak at heart. I mentioned before that I am a realist. Meaning, I don't sugar coat shyt.

In this book I will have cusswords, typos and words spelled my way instead of the English Dictionary. There is a time and a place for everything and this is not a college term paper. I feel no need to be politically correct. I will use my slang freely. I will give you the real, unabridged edition raw and uncut.

I will give you positive and motivating quotes from lifes greatest teachers and some pulled from The Bible itself. I am not limiting the quotes used from just females, we will also learn from some of our most amazing male counterparts. **Women empowerment is not about degrading Men.** Both heroes and she-roes will be acknowledged in this book.

I give out very little relationship advice. A young woman's focus should be on her own personal success. Always put yourself and your children first. If you have children, make sure those children are taken care of. Men are always a distant second. Think of them as a leisure activity for you to do after you have accomplished all your goals for the day. **Still respect men, but respect yourself, your goals, and your children more.**

You will have favorite rules; you will have least favorite rules. You may not feel me on every point, but rally with me on others. Some of the rules may sound like I'm talking to you directly.

From one Bad Bytch to another, I AM. I may not know your situation directly, but I know what you're going through. My feet have been in your shoes ladies. It took me years of experience in many different situations to write each rule in this book. I learned through trial and error what it takes to get on top.

I have studied the work of the greatest and have organized the information I received, the best I could in a step by step, rule by rule collection. For those that do not yet know the way, I am lighting it up and pointing out the right direction.

For my sisters whom are already on the right path, I hope this book gives you tips and helps you solidify what you are already doing. If any portions of this book sound unclear to you at first. Hang in there with it! I promise that it will all make sense in the end. The most vital important information you will see get repeated several times throughout the book.

Please understand when I say **B.A.D B.Y.T.C.H.** I simply mean **B**eautiful **A**nd **D**etermined in **B**ring **Y**our **T**hinking **C**onstantly **H**igher. I took a term that the hip hop community uses to describe attractive and successful women and Im using it in the most positive way.

Do not let the word offend you. **Remember, being a Bad Bytch it is not all about looks. It is about having the proper mentality that will help you achieve your goals.**

I believe in respecting women of all Nationalities, Sexual Preferences, Religions and any or all differences. Understand The word "Bytch" is being used in the most positive and respectful way as humanely possibly. Do not let it scare you.

PROCEED with **CAUTION** !!

"....man looks on the outward appearance, but the Lord looks on the heart."

— 1 Samuel 16:7

My Reasons

A little about me, each rule is based off a situation I experienced on my path to success. I am the self-appointed Bad Bytch Lieutenant. I will be making General here very soon. My resume is impeccable. Everything I talk about, I speak from experience.

I have two college degrees, several properties and my own successful business. I am self-made, educated, successful and sexy. I have beaten every stereo type and make more money than the majority of most white men. More importantly I am a young minority woman and I'm out here doing it.

I tend to lash out at the younger generation coming up right now, but I am doing so in the most loving big sisterly way that I can. I am a female whom looks like you, talks like you and been in many of the same situations you have been before. I wish someone had taken the time to write me out a guide book to help me out through life and difficult situations.

Quite frankly, I wrote this book to help out any sister out there who has lost there way and needs the path to light up for them. Also I would like to help out the legion of women whom are already on the right path but would like confirmation that what they are doing is correct.

This book is to create a support system for women like you. When you are a BAD BYTCH, you will meet opposition. I refer to this opposition as rat whores, but you can create your own term for them.

Every day, we as women are given opportunities to make our own choices. One direction you could chose to go is the LIGHT, POSITIVE, GOOD, LOVING, and SUPPORTIVE. The other direction is DARK, NEGATIVE, EVIL, JEALOUS, CONFUSING and not beneficial to anyone. I am drawing definite lines in the sand. Pick which side you are on.

You have been warned; now continue on if you dare…..

BAD BYTCH RULE NO. 1: Keep your mind and your eyes on your muthafukkin money.

"The lack of money is the root of all evil." – Mark Twain

Memorize this rule. It is number one for a reason. Distractions are all over the place. Sometimes they come disguised as friends, sometimes they are tall dark and handsome. We live in a society based upon numbers. These numbers will decide where you live, how you live and more importantly your children's future. Of course, we will want these numbers piled up and on our side. Watch your numbers like a muthafukkin hawk. **When someone tries to distract you, recognize it and stay focused.**

Do I like money? Not really. It has started way too many disputes, burnt too many bridges and started too much war fare. Do I know I need it to survive? Yes. No skating around it. That's what makes me a Hustler. In our society, Money is needed to survive. Once you understand that, go a little deeper.

Realize that many must live in poverty, for few to live in luxury. Statistics show that less than 4% of the world's population controls over 96% of the world's money. While the rest of us just struggle and scramble trying to make it. We scam one another trying to get it. Where do you think that the 4% that control the worlds money live at? Do you think they live in your neighborhood? Think again! However, they do love for you to live in that neighborhood and fight and steal from one another just for basic survival. Now that we have established the facts what are we going to do?

A true Bad Bytch will try and change those percentages to be more in her favor. You can either work to join up with the 4%, or you can kick a muthafukkin hole in that statistic and make your own damn statistics!

Change your mentality. To have money like them, first we have to think like them. The information is out there, however the wealthy count on our ignorance to either not to seek out the information or to receive the information and not use it.

Over consuming is the biggest obstacle to overcome to become wealthy. Do you know what you can afford on your salary? Do you even know what your salary is? Smarten up ladies! The first step is figuring out how much money you bring in on a day to day basis. Then, figure it up for weekly, monthly, and yearly. Write this down in your financial journal or invest in a good computer program that will store the information for you.

Always know exactly how much money you are working with. Know your bank account balances at all times. Know how much money you have in your wallet. Access how much of it is for spending and how much is for bills.

To start you off I will give you a simple formula. Once you have calculated how much you are working with, you use a budget plan to calculate how much you should be spending in which areas. Total debt and monthly bills should be under 50% of your income. Approximately 35% of your income should be mortgage/rent and utility bills. The other 15% should be car, insurance, and ugh... credit card bills. Now this is just a simple formula to get your started. Once you begin to study money, you will find deeper more complex equations that will break it down even more for you.

Be very careful for being an over consumer. The money you spend in a night club, out to eat, on clothing, expensive cars etc. can easily get you in debt and in trouble. Learning how to live off less money and saving more may be frustrating at first, but it is a definite necessity in changing your life for the better.

Every penny that you save is going to bring you closer to the 4%. It gives you a security blanket for unexpected expenses and allows you to invest into your dreams! Keep your eyes on your muthafukkin money ladies! It will change your life!

"In all realms of life it takes courage to stretch your limits, express your power, and fullfill your potential... it's no different in the financial realm."

— Suze Orman

BAD BYTCH RULE NO. 2: Never ever, ever, ever fight with a Hater. We love our Haters, they are FREE PROMOTION!

"Today is Hater Day. Everyone please let them get their 2 minutes of fame and light! I Love You Haters. Continue to make me proud of u guys! "
— Lebron James

A Hater is really a fan whom is confused. All the time that a hater devotes to researching you, investigating you and even bad mouthing you is a strong investment in your future success. Welcome your haters with as much love and support as you welcome your supporters. Why would you fight with them? You have already defeated them. They are taking the time out of their empty lives to devote to you.

Experts tell us that the best type of promotion out there is word of mouth. Anyone that is talking about you, whether it is good or bad, is promoting you and your brand. It will cause others to become curious about you and try to figure out who you are. Not everyone that they refer to you will have a hater a$$ opinion. They might even point out to the hater that they in fact are hating.

A millionaire once told me that you can measure your success off the number of haters you have. My experience has shown me that this is true. If you don't believe me just look at any one who has experienced high levels of success. You will find critics all over the place.

A Bad Bytch should gladly accept constructive criticism from a person whom is more spiritually advanced or someone whom makes more money than them. Anyone else is more than likely a hater. Don't let a haters negativity get you down at all. Make sure you thank them for their time and attention. Smile pretty for your haters and keep it moving. Pray that one day they will learn to love themselves, so they don't have to hate you so much.

"Hate is too great a burden to bear. It injures the hater more than it injures the hated."

– Coretta Scott King

BAD BYTCH RULE NO. 3: **When you see another BAD BYTCH throw up the proper salutation. Leave the hating up to the Basic Bytchez.**

"Hating someone will not make you any prettier!"

— Kimora Lee

This is what separates the Women from the Hoes. One Bad Bytch should never feel threatened by another one. We are of the some breed. When one Bad Bytch is doing well, it opens up doors for other Bad Bytchez to get through. If you have your own career, your own life and own dreams that you are pursuing, then you know how difficult the path to success can be. When you see another female whom is out there doing their thing, be proud and show a mutual respect for that. If you show the proper amount of Love and Respect, there are possibilities of networking and doing business together in the future.

If you still hate on another woman, then you are still developing at a very basic mentality. Remember our fight is not with each other. We are just out here to try to make some money and survive. Statistics show that less than 4% of the world controls 96% of the world's money. To make enemies with one of your own kind is foolish and basic. Let's go at the muthafukkas that got all the money and ain't trying to share it.

Inevitably, one day you may cross paths with another Bad Bytch in an unfriendly situation. Maybe y'all messed with the same person. Or maybe y'all are in the same line of work and there is a little competition thing. A Bad Bytch should be polished enough to behave like a mature adult. You may not do business with her, but still throw up the proper salute. **Respect her hustle if you want her to respect yours.**

Please remember that BAD BYTCHEZ come in all shapes, colors, and sizes. It is more about the MENTALITY than anything else! Some of the most beautiful women have the mentality of a very basic whore. Don't be fooled by a cute hoodrat pretending to be a Bad Bytch. Never overlook a sister who's appearance you don't think fits the profile. Her mentality and business could be super on point.

"Ladies when you see a beautiful woman compliment her even if you feel insecure. Do it! You'll feel good"

— Amber Rose

BAD BYTCH RULE NO. 4: Block out negativity on any level and in any form of it. You know your path. Stay on it and stay focused.

"I want to fight poverty and ignorance and give opportunity to those people who are locked out." – Russell Simmons

Negativity will come at you from all angles and from places you will never expect it. You have to rebuke all negativity just like you would rebuke the devil. What God has for you, no one can take from you but yourself. It is up to you to become very clear about what you want out of life and pursue it! Focus is key. Learn to block out negative energy and stay tuned to the positive.

Now this is when you need to look at your inner circle. Determine whom is bringing negativity and drama into your life. I promise you this, if success does not change you, it will most definitely change the people around you. It is very important to surround yourself with people whom are motivated, positive and like-minded. If you have someone around you whom is filling your life with drama, criticism or negativity of any kind it is time to re-evaluate their position in your life.

"It takes much bravery to stand up to our enemies but we need as much bravery to stand up to our friends."
— J.K. Rowling

BAD BYTCH RULE NO.5: Education is Power. Education is Key!! Don't get Jerked. Always educate yourself in the classroom and the streets.

"I've always liked my women book and street smart.

As long as they gotta little class like half days

And the confidence to overlook my past ways."

– Drake

How many times to you pay someone to do something for you simply because you don't know how to do it yourself. From the mechanic, the plumber, the editor, the promoter, they are all making money off your lack of education in their field. I am not saying to learn every trade there is. However, I am saying learn enough about that field to make a good decision. Never appear to be clueless or misinformed. Know what the value of their service is. Figure out exactly how it is going to benefit you. Find out what a fair price for their service should be. Do your research on them prior to employing them. Get several quotes for the same service. We live in a society where information is at your fingertips. Educate yourself in various subjects so when you go in to a situation you know what's going on!

Achieve personal education throughout your life. College degrees, classes, certifications will all give you value. They increase your ability to make more money. Whatever your field is, becoming an expert in it. Hang up your degrees and diplomas proudly!

Education on the streets is totally different. You can either be a hustler or you can get hustled. This is especially for my ladies, in the modeling, music or entertainment industry. **There are scams everywhere. There are people looking for someone undereducated in their field so they can take advantage of you. Don't get jerked Ladies!** Be informed! Research every venture, do background checks, verify people and the claims they make before doing business with them. Nowadays, there are more CEO's than there are businesses. Everyone got a side hustle. Just don't get jerked by a side hustle that is not legit.

"Education is the most powerful weapon which you can use to change the world."

— Nelson Mandela

BAD BYTCH RULE NO. 6: Not everyone is your friend. There are some true snakes out there. Keep your eyes wide open and your grass cut real low.

"An insincere and evil friend is more to be feared than a wild beast; a wild beast may wound your body, but an evil friend will wound your mind."

– Buddha

Pay attention very closely to this rule. We call them snakes because they are sneaky. They have very clever ways of disguising themselves and making it on to your front lawn before you even see their true intentions.

Have you ever randomly met a female randomly and she befriends you. You may have a lot in common with her, or so you think. Then it all turns out that y'all know the same people and she knew exactly who you were in the first place? She even planned out the meeting and everything. Sounds very single white female right? Im telling you right now it happens. Very little happens by coincidence.

The "modeling scout" that just approached you randomly at an event, he could have been watching you for a long time now and following your career. While some people are harmless and truly are there to help you, be aware that some are out to get you. There are male snakes, female snakes, and the will have several different tactics to get to you. Never let them catch you slipping. Keep your eyes wide open.

When someone is properly ID'd as a snake, be aware the only proper way to kill a snake is off with their head. Sever all ties with them swiftly and immediately in a way that will ensure they will never come back.

"He who passively accepts evil is as much involved in it as he who helps to perpetrate it. He who accepts evil without protesting against it is really cooperating with it."

– Martin Luther King, Jr.

BAD BYTCH RULE NO. 7: **Keep yourself right spiritually. Know who and what you believe in. Know your morals and stick to them.**

"We've all got both light and dark inside us. What matters is the part we choose to act on. That's who we really are."

— J.K. Rowling

Evil is no illusion. Every single day we all get up with a choice to make. Our choices can lead us on a righteous path, closer to our goals and closer to success. Those choices are good choices and are considered light. While another set of choices could harm us and harm others. It is mean-spirited, jealous and negative. It may give us temporary happiness, yet will hurt you in the long run. These choices are bad and considered dark. Everyday each one of us has opportunities to make "Light" Choices or "Dark Choices". This is the very definition of Good Vs. Evil. Decide which side you will serve.

Make sure you choices clearly represent the intentions of your heart. You set your own morals. It's up to you to live up to them. Quietly consider your options. Decide which choices support you living the best life possible.

"for I am persuaded, that neither death, nor life, nor angels, nor principalities, nor powers, nor things present, nor things to come, Nor height, nor depth, nor any other creature, shall be able to separate us from the love of God, which is in Christ Jesus our Lord."

— Romans 8:38, 39

BAD BYTCH RULE NO. 8: Loyalty is Everything. A loyal team is a magnificent accomplishment. If someone shows signs of disloyalty handle it harshly and immediately.

"When you have a good friend that really cares for you and tries to stick in there with you, you treat them like nothing. Learn to be a good friend because one day you're gonna look up and say I lost a good friend. Learn how to be respectful to your friends, don't just start arguments with them and don't tell them the reason, always remember your friends will be there quicker than your family. Learn to remember you got great friends, don't forget that and they will always care for you no matter what. Always remember to smile and look up at what you got in life."

— Marilyn Monroe

What does loyalty mean to you? This is a very important question to ask yourself.

What do you expect of your team? Can you get on the same page with them? Is there cooperation? A person's loyalty is more valuable than money. **With strong, loyal partners you can make a million a, million different ways, a million times over.** With disloyal partners, everyone would be lying to each other and stealing from one another until the partnership is in the dust.

Chose your team wisely. Put them through a series of situations to verify their loyalty. Determine if this person even loyal to themselves, their goals, their commitments? A female or male whom is disloyal to themselves will rarely be loyal to you. They are still developing on beginner level.

Disloyalty is suicide. It's the end of the partnership. No longer continue in a business or personal relationship with someone whom is disloyal. This person can no longer be trusted. Their intentions are unknown and they are lower than the snakes.

"Be slow to fall into friendship; but when thou art in, continue firm and constant."

–Socrates

BAD BYTCH RULE NO. 9: Never take your eyes off the end result. Keep your eyes on the prize. Non-Believers will be converted with RESULTS.

"This is one small step for a man, one giant leap for mankind."

_ Neil Armstrong

You have a goal that you have set for yourself. Keep your faith that you can and will achieve your goal. There may be troubles along the way, but with every issue there is always a solution. It may not be as easy as you thought it was, but you will steady make progress. Just always keep your goal on your mind.

Use anything in your power to help you stay focused and motivated. Seek mentors. Create a vision board. Journal your goals and track your progress. When a person doubts that you will reach your goal, don't become angry, become motivated. When your naysayers see your results, they will be converted into supporters. **Always keep your faith.**

"Keep your eyes on the prize and don't turn back."

– Bill Clinton

BAD BYTCH RULE NO. 10: Always take security measures. Keep a velvet glove over an iron fist. Respect is a MUST.

"Before all else, be armed." – Niccolo Machiavelli

More money, more problems. We better believe it. Success breeds enemies. Yes, it is unfortunate, but it is true. This is the point where a lot of women will fold. A true Bad Bytch will stand her ground.

Security is a major part of the game. Think personal security. Some of us Bad Bytchez have made it to a level of success where security and body guards are needed. Obtaining your CCW Permits is also highly recommended. Never travel alone. Set your alarm. Always make sure your home is secure. Now switch to thinking of security in much bigger terms.

Have you made sure you had proper legal representation review all your contracts and other aspects of your business? I cannot stress the importance of having your paperwork right and in order. Make sure you obtain the proper licenses and trademarks. Always have your files backed up.

If you Model, own the rights to your pictures. Free photo shoots may sound like a good deal, but it usually means you don't own the rights to your pictures.

If you do music get your final copy of every song BDS certified and copy-written. Know your rights and keep your business secure at all times. People will show you respect when they see you are serious. Keep yourself and your business completely secure at all times.

Now there is a catch to this. A Bad Bytch MUST be able to accomplish complete security, while maintaining a calm, cool and collective image. No one wants to network with a complete total bytch that's constantly spazing out.

You MUST maintain a friendly, professional and approachable image. However, be overly prepared that if a situation arises, whether it is physical altercation or legal matter, stand your ground and emerge the winner.

"For to win one hundred victories in one hundred battles is not the acme of skill. To subdue the enemy without fighting is the acme of skill."

– Sun Tzu

BAD BYTCH RULE NO. 11: Love and Respect the twatty. A clean kitty is a happy kitty..keep it clean and well groomed. Keep the miles off your pu$$y and disease free.

"One must not make oneself cheap here – that is a cardinal point – or else one is done. Whoever is most impertinent has the best chance."

– Wolfgang Amadeus Mozart

Be proud of your pu$$y and treat her very good. Low miles and regular maintenance is highly suggested. Whether your prefer Brazilian waxes or landing strips, be sure to keep her well groomed for best performances.

For some this rule may come easy, however there are some ladies whom abuse and neglect their kitties. You gotta boss that pu$$y game up at all costs. Messing around intimately with lames is a huge no-no. Being intimate with strangers is a **HELL NO**!

ALWAYS **protect** yourself and your kitty!! Keep the strange dick away. Get tested regularly for STD's and maintain your birth control. Take complete responsibility for your own proper pu$$y maintenance and keeping high standards for yourself.

"Bad bytchez do not have promiscuous sex."

– Nicki Minaj

BAD BYTCH RULE NO. 12: Keep them raggedy ass, confused, weak ass bytchez OFF your team. Real recognize Real!

"The shyt you hear might be true but then again, it could be as fake as the bytchez who told you."

– Lil Wayne

It happens to the best of us. Somehow, some way a raggedy bytch might sneak her way on to your team. She may preach that she wants change in her life, but then you notice she keeps making the same stupid a$$ decisions. She stays complaining, but keeps fuckin with the same losers. Was she bullshytting you from the start? Is she just weak or is she confused about what she really wants.

More importantly, who got the time to sit there and try to figure someone else the fukk out? Whatever her issue is, once she has been properly identified, be sure to get her up off your team as soon as possible. Life is too short for the bullshytters. Don't go insane fuckin with her a$$. Recognize real women when you see them.

Your team will only be as strong as the weakest link on your team. Know where the weakness is coming from. Make a choice to either burden yourself with their extra weight or make them hold their own. Make choices that protect the strength and longevity of your team.

There are women who wonder through life in a state of confusion. Then we also women whom are completely confused about what team they want to be on. Hoes switch teams more than NBA players do and it aint due to the draft. Be prepared to defend yourself against these ruthless women. Hoes are disloyal as fuck and when you see the weakness in them address is quickly and immediately.

"I don't even call it violence when it's in self defense; I call it intelligence."

– Malcolm X

BAD BYTCH RULE NO. 13: Don't let your pu$$Y join the Miles High Club. Being known as a homie smasher will trash your reputation.

"Hoes want attention, women want respect."
– Drake

Soo many attractive women have fell in this trap. We all know a female whom is attractive and always seems to be on the scene. Whatever club is slappin, or whatever performer is in town, she's in there and you can bet on that. Personality is a plus and she's social so she gets several men hollering at her. Over time, a few may succeed in getting to her. They may fuck around for a couple weeks, then lose interest or have a falling. Next thing you know, one of his dudes is now trying to holler at her. He swear he's different. He got every line in the book he's using. Next thing you know, she's smashing the homie.

Believe me ladies, men talk. Men gossip more than women nowadays. If the dude you currently are dating has a friend that you slept with, it's just a matter of time before he finds out about it.

Just a few months hanging out in the same clubs and in the same cities and you will have a few different fellaz that can claim they hit that. Next thing you know, people will start with that "oh yeah she's cute, but everyone done fucked her." Once women catch that label it is almost impossible to bounce back from it. This is a main reason why young ladies are randomly locating to different areas, where their reputation isn't known yet.

It doesn't take long and it doesn't take a lot to trash your reputation. Ladies, treasure your reputation. Fucking with multiple men in the same crew is a super no no, especially if you want them to take you seriously.

"It takes 20 years to build a reputation and five minutes to ruin it. If you think about that, you'll do things differently."
—Warren Buffett

BAD BYTCH RULE NO. 14: Spend a little cash on your shoes and purses. A Gucci purse can make a tank top look high fashion.

"Sunglasses, my diamond earrings, and my watch. I wear that with everything."

— Amber Rose

A woman with a true sense of style can go to a second hand store and come out looking like a million dollars. It's not always about the clothes, its more about the woman in the clothes.

Cheap, trendy clothes will go in and out of fashion, but a few high end accessories will always be stylish.

When it comes to a **Bad Bytch's** wardrobe, the most money should always be invested into your shoes, purses, glasses and jewelry. A high end designer purse can make your gym clothes look classy. A nice pair of designer heels can make your $5 leggings look like couture. Invest in pieces that will be timeless and will take you everywhere from a concert to a business meeting.

Remember Bad Bytchez, shoes strings are only for the gym, or for running errands. When you are stepping out or in a professional setting, no shoes with shoe strings are allowed.

"That is the key of this collection, being yourself. Don't be into trends. Don't make fashion own you, but you decide what you are, what you want to express by the way you dress and the way to live."
— Gianni Versace

BAD BYTCH RULE NO. 15: Always have your own money, but PREFER to spend his!!!!

"Last year my wife got a Rolls-Royce."

— Russel Simmons

A true **Bad Bytch** will always keep her on stacks. We might be stacking it and saving it, but we will always have our own. A smart women, will get money from all angles. Never limit yourself to just one hustle.

When it comes to male companions, making a man match you is not gold digging. It's the bare minimum. Make sure your man can match your motivation, drive and money. Make sure his a$$ ain't selfish with it either.

A Bad Bytch likes to be spoiled by our male counterpart. We work long hard days chasing our dreams. Our mentality is completely different than the next bytch. Our behavior is completely different than the next bytch. So you better treat us better than the next bytch. That means we deserve nice things, quality time and romance.

Ladies, make sure your man is doing things for you because he wants to and not because you need it. **There a big difference when someone buys you something because they want you to have it versus when they buy it for you because you cannot provide it for yourself. Always be able to stand on your own two. Watch the level of respect a man will show you when he knows you can provide for yourself.**

Behind every King, there is an equally intelligent, strong Queen playing her position well. Queens require love and special attention. Letting your man spoil you isn't hoeing. You're a Bad Bytch, you deserve it!

"I'm here to tell you, though, ladies that the term "gold digger" is one of the traps we men set to keep you off our money trail; we created that term for you so that we can have all our money and still get everything we want from you without you asking for or expecting this very basic, instinctual responsibility that men all over the world are obligated to assume and embrace. ... KNOW THIS: It is your right to expect that a man will pay for your dinner, your movie ticket, your club entry fee, or whatever else he has to pay for in exchange for your time."

— Steve Harvey

BAD BYTCH RULE NO. 16: Your body is indeed a temple. Exercise hard and exercise often. Keep yourself HEALTHY and emotionally stable.

"There are many aspects to success; material wealth is only one component. ...But success also includes good health, energy and enthusiasm for life, fulfilling relationships, creative freedom, emotional and psychological stability, a sense of well-being, and peace of mind."

— Deepak Chopra

Get active!! The human body is an amazing gift from God. Treat your body as a temple and keep it in tip top condition. Let Healthy Habits follow you through life. Women with active life styles are more likely to aggressively pursue their goals. Inactivity and procrastination can negatively impact your ability to achieve your goals.

Keep your days as active as possible! At least 30minutes of cardio every single day is a good place to start. This can be as simple as cleaning your house at a fast pace or just walking regularly. Find an activity that you love and can commit to.

Pay very close attention to what you put inside your body for nutrition. Diets can be hard and frustrating. Practice healthy eating habits instead. Drink plenty of water every single day. Eat plenty of fruits and vegetables. Limit the amount of fast food that your family consumes. Instead, make regular trips to the grocery store. Prepare you and your families meals yourself. That way you can control what goes into them. Allow yourself to enjoy your favorites, but as with anything, practice limitations.

Keep yourself healthy inside and out. Learn how to quiet your mind and meditate daily. Know who and what you believe in. Be very aware of your energy and emotions. Keep everything on a positive wave length as much as possible.

"The physical and emotional health of an entire generation and the economic health and security of our nation is at stake. This isn't the kind of problem that can be solved overnight, but with everyone working together, it can be solved. So, let's move."
–Michelle Obama 'The First Lady'

BAD BYTCH RULE NO. 17: Never expect LOYALTY from a bytch that isn't even loyal to herself. AVOID THESE TYPE BYTCHEZ AT ALL COSTS!

"Self-Made, You Just Affiliated I Build The Ground Up, You Bought And Renovated Talking Plenty Capers, Nothings Been Authenticated Funny You Claiming The Same Bytch That I'm Penetrating."

— Rick 'Rozay' Ross

Loyalty starts at home. It always starts with **self**. Have you made a commitment to set and achieve goals for yourself? Do the people around you pursue their goals with the same drive and determination as you do? If not they can slow you down. If you encounter someone who is not even loyal to her own goals, her own beliefs, her own claims, she will never be loyal to you. You will be wasting your time.

It is never enough to just claim a belief on a certain subject, but you have to consistently live as such. Never let your mouth write checks that you're a$$ can't cash. If you claim that you are down with a certain team or certain morals be prepared to live up to it.

If you notice someone whom is disloyal to herself and the choices she has made in life, be very aware that she will show you the same disloyalty in your life. It's best to keep her at a distance.

"Some chicks are only as loyal as their next photo shoot, video or magazine layout!"

– DJ Kay Slay Owner Straight Stuntin Magazine

BAD BYTCH RULE NO. 18: Karma is the Baddest Bytch of them all!!! STAY ON HER GOOD SIDE!

"For what shall it profit a man, if he shall gain the whole world, and lose his own soul?"

— Mark 8:36

Karma is real. Karma is perfect. It is God's Law. It can be very beautiful if you allow it to be. Always be aware of how you treat other people. Everything that you say and do to each other is being recorded. You will reciprocate the same energy that you put out there. Whether it is good or bad is up to you. **The Golden Rule is to do unto others, as you would have them do unto you.**

You can chose to spread around good energy and good karma or you can chose to treat people poorly. Choose wisely and knowing that you will have to meet any karma that you put out there.

You may think that no one knows that you did this or maybe you think you may have got away with that, but Karma always knows and she will always come for you. Do yourself a favor and stay on her good side!

"The recognition of the law of the cause and effect, also known as karma, is a fundamental key to understand how you've created your world, with actions of your body, speech and mind. When you truly understand karma, then you realize you are responsible for everything in your life. It is incredibly empowering to know that your future is in your hands."

— Keanu Reeves

BAD BYTCH RULE NO. 19: **BUILD YOUR HOUSE WITH BRICKS so when these ugly ass wolf lookin bytchez come blowing everything, your house won't budge.**

"A house divided against itself cannot stand."

– Abraham Lincoln

We all know what happened with the three little pigs. Don't let your house cave in on you. Start with a solid foundation and slowly and carefully put each brick in its place. There are women whom simply have zero respect for themselves. There are women who will make it their business every single day to fuck with you and try to fuck up what you have going on. Whether its hating, whether its jealously, whatever their motive is, be prepared for these ugly bytchez and their ugly ways.

A home that is securely built on a solid foundation won't move in inch when these desperate hoes show up. Ensure that your household will survive and storm that may blow through.

"A house is not a home unless it contains food and fire for the mind as well as the body."

– Benjamin Franklin

BAD BYTCH RULE NO. 20: Always keep the ball in your court. Know the Game in all aspects and play it very well.

"I play to win, whether during practice or a real game. And I will not let anything get in the way of me and my competitive enthusiasm to win."
- Michael Jordan

If you decide to get into the game, you must know all the rules. Obey the rules, or don't play the game. Know whom your key players are. Never fumble or drop the ball. Keep the ball in your court and under your control.

A good rule of thumb is to try to become an absolute expert in your field. Whatever your gift is, or whatever it is that you chose to pursue in life, absolutely attempt to Master it. Become the very best at it. Always show good sportsman like conduct. Welcome friendly competition. Practice and preparation will keep your team on top.

"I've learned that you shouldn't go through life with a catcher's mitt on both hands; you need to be able to throw something back."
- Maya Angelou

BAD BYTCH RULE NO. 21: **WRITE DOWN EVERYTHING GOALS AND ACCOMPLISHMENTS! Keep a diary of all your goals. Adjust them and track progress daily.**

"Ask, and it shall be given you; seek, and ye shall find; knock, and it shall be opened unto you."

— Matthew 7:7

Don't be afraid to ask for what you want in life. Become very clear about what it is that you want. **There is power in your own hand writing.** Invest in a good journal. Invest in pens that you love to write with, whether its smooth ink or wild unique colors. Keep track of everything from schedules to appointments to your goals and accomplishments.

It is one thing to think it, however to write it down and start planning it is what makes your dreams come alive. Feel free to update and adjust your goals as needed. Be proud of all your accomplishments and keep track of everything that you achieve.

If you are ever feeling down or just need to vent, try writing a letter to God. I promise you, it helps.

"Everyone has inside of her a piece of good news. The good news is that you don't know how great you can be! How much you can love! What you can accomplish! And what your potential is!"

— Anne Frank

BAD BYTCH RULE NO. 22: Let jealous bytchez be jealous bytchez. Never waste your precious time worrying about the next bytch. Focus on your prosperity.

"If the world hate you, ye know that it hated me before it hated you."

— ST John 15:18

Any type of success will breed envy. Jealously is a very deep rooted sickness and it is very contagious. Focusing on your own future and success is the only known antidote. Never spend one minute of your life worried about the next bytch. Always focus on yourself and achieving your own goals. You could spend 100% of your time working, going to school and just taking care of your family and you will have women that hate you for no reason. Let them be jealous. Work hard and let the hoes hate you for it.

A jealous bytch will have many different ways that they will try to take you out of focus. Simply ask yourself if this person's actions or opinions have a direct impact on the amount of money that you are able to bring into your household. If the answer is No, then their negativity should be ignored. As long as they are not hurting you or your family, let them hate all day. You simply cannot please everyone, nor should you waste your time trying to. The very moment that you stop giving a fukk about what another person has to say about you, your life will get better. Your time is very precious, don't waste one second addressing negativity. Keep it positive and keep it moving.

They say money is the root of all jealousy. I believe it is more appropriate to say that insecurity is in the root of all jealousy. Be jealous of another woman for what? **You have absolutely no idea what they had to do to get where they are at.** If you see something there that you want for yourself, you need to set a goal and work towards it. A true Bad Bytch would never waste any moment of time hating on the next bytch. For what? **We can achieve whatever we set our mind out to achieve.**

If you see jealousy, nip it in the bud. It is a sickness and it is very contagious. I have seen whole crews of women that operate on negativity and jealously. Shame on their asses! They are destined for failure. Spend less time keeping track of what someone else got going on and make your own achievements. Focus on yourself and your own prosperity.

"Do not overrate what you have received, nor envy others. He who envies others does not obtain peace of mind."

– Buddha

BAD BYTCH RULE NO. 23: A relationship should be similar to the merger of two major corporations with both parties bringing a lot to the table.

"I think it takes a special man to be with a certain kind of a woman, and I think that for me, I look for someone is strong. I feel like my husband is very strong, distinguished, very sexy, very humble, very sweet, very loving, and I think that whatever it is that you like in a relationship, you should look for that in a relationship."

— Kimora Lee

Perfect relationships don't exist. Perfect partnerships do. There has to be compromises made and each party has to learn to adapt to one another. Physical attraction is just the first step to a happy relationship. To obtain true satisfaction with your mate look deeper into their mentality. What does this person have going on for themselves and what is their future plans. How do their goals and achievements impact your own.

Your partner can be your partner in many different ways. Is it ever enough to be simply satisfied with good looks and good sex? Take a close look at the bigger picture of compatibility. Do you and your mate have similar goals and interest? Do you help motivate and support one another throughout life? Looking deeper than just physical attraction is what builds power couples like Jay Z and Beyoncé.

For longevity, seek out relationships which bring your life happiness and fulfillment. Be your partners friend first. Learn to respect one another. Respect each other's dreams. Be able to enlighten and encourage each other. **A true Bad Bytch will ensure that their partner will help transform their life for the better.**

"Don't make me laugh boo

Never did that bad to

Make you even have to

But even if I had to

Ask my better half to

You be more than glad to

When I do that math boo

You always try to add two"

– Fabolous

BAD BYTCH RULE NO. 24: **Some people are still developing at a beginner levels. Helping them is good, but never let them slow down your advancement to higher levels.**

"On many long journeys have I gone. And waited, too, for others to return from journeys of their own. Some return; some are broken; some come back so different only their names remain."

— Yoda

There is a fine line between offering someone a helping hand and completely doing it for them. There will be people whom take kindness for weakness and expect you to do everything for them. It is good to help out, but don't get caught up in pursuing someone else's goals for them. You should never have to plan out someone else's life and guide them through it step by step. Offer help when you can, but never let someone rely completely on you to do everything for them.

Don't slow your own progress down to allow someone else to catch up to your advancement. That can turn into you carrying their weight also. When you have to carry other people through it can slow down your own advancements. There are people who want and deserve help and there are others whom will simply eat up all your time and attention. Always stay focused on your goals and dreams.

"I got these haters

Like when will he

stop, Maybe a

minute after never

so set your clocks"

— Lil Wayne

BAD BYTCH RULE NO. 25: It is much better to have someone's RESPECT rather than their SYMPATHY. Play on people's emotions but not to the extreme.

"If you don't respect nothin' else, you will respect this hustle."

  — T.I.

We all know someone whom will tell you sob story after sob story in attempts to get attention and sympathy. They use people's sympathy to get what they want out of life. **It is much, much better to have someone's respect than their sympathy.** Playing on someone's emotions can totally backfire on you. They may feel sympathetic at the moment, but decide not to do business with you because you are overly emotional.

Learn to master your emotions. Emotions have absolutely no place in business. No matter what you are going through at home, make sure you check it in at the door when you are in a professional setting. Emotions can cloud judgment and you must be able to think clearly in a working environment.

Let people respect you for your hard work. Let people respect you for your achievements. Let these muthafukkaz know that they don't have to like you, but they will respect you. A true Bad Bytch got more hustle than a little bit.

"I learned something from that. If someone asks me something that I really don't want to do, I say no. I have to trust that. And I'm not afraid to talk money."

- Diana Ross

BAD BYTCH RULE NO. 26: Seek out mentors and like-minded people. Value their time and absorb all the information and motivation they are willing to give you.

"How important it is for us to recognize and celebrate our heroes and she-roes!"
—Maya Angelou

A female with a highly developed intellect will come to love and appreciate the masters in her field. A mentor is someone whom has already went through what you are going through and has come out successful. They will be able to pass along tips and secrets that will help you along your way. Seek out quality mentors in your field. Make sure you value their time. They did not become successful by wasting time. If they agree to guide you or meet with you, make sure you are appreciative and show up on time and ready to learn. Absorb and consider all the information they are willing to pass along to you.

If you are unable to connect personally with a mentor, you may be able to still learn from them through books or social networking. Seek out positive, like-minded people that you can vibe with and learn from.

Study all the Greats in history. When looking for life's greatest teachers, a great place to start would be to familiarize yourself with all the Nobel Prize winners. Also, research all the women pioneers. Try to learn their traits and habits that led them to success. Celebrate our legends and left them motivate and influence your work!

"It's better to hang out with people better than you. Pick out associates whose behavior is better than yours and you'll drift in that direction."
— Warren Buffett

BAD BYTCH RULE NO. 27: Never expect RESPECT from a female whom doesn't RESPECT herself.

"If we are to go forward, we must go back and rediscover those precious values – that all reality hinges on moral foundations and that all reality has spiritual control."
– Martin Luther King, Jr.

There are women that have made it to adulthood, but never developed a sense of self-respect. I don't know whether to blame them or to blame it on her momma. If you encounter a woman with little or no respect for themselves, keep them away from your inner circle. She will never respect you or anything that you have going on for yourself. Respect, is like Loyalty and it starts within self.

A woman with no self-respect is like a ticking time bomb waiting to explode. Keep your distance from her, so you, your career and your household will not be impacted negatively from her life choices.

"You gotta be a beast. That's the only way they'll respect you."
– Nicki Minaj

BAD BYTCH RULE NO. 28: If you cannot effectively maintain and properly manage your own Pu$$y, then you could never run your own company. Better Boss that Pu$$y game up.

"Only make decisions that support your self-image, self-worth, and self-esteem."

— Oprah Winfrey

How many successful female CEO's do you know that are complete whores. Stop and really think about this. How many significant others can you even place Oprah with. **A Bad Bytch is a boss and is in control in every situation. Rarely, do you see a woman whose sex life is out of control, but money is on point. If you want to own and manage your own company you need organization and self-control.**

When you are in a powerful position, you have to ensure that there is a high level of respect for you in your field. It will be impossible to receive respect from others, if you don't even have that respect for yourself.

Famous whores routinely end up running through their money just as quick that men run through their pu$$y. Not to mention the majority of whores also suffer from emotional issues, drug dependencies and other downfalls of their self-abuse.

If a female can't even properly maintain and manage their own pu$$y, then how could they ever branch out and manage anything else effectively? Stay bossed up in all aspects.

"Do not leave your reputation to chance or gossip; it is your life's artwork, and you must craft it, hone it, and display it with the care of an artist."
— Robert Greene

BAD BYTCH RULE NO. 29: True genuine supporters are rare. Be prepared to hold your own.

"The reason I want to be alone, is I'm tired of all the things that went wrong that would've went right if I had did 'em on my own" — Nas

True and genuine supporters are a rare find this day in age. Be prepared to hold your own in every situation, even if no one else supports your cause. Be able to operate completely independently of others. Keep the control in your hands to make powerful decisions without assistance. Be able to finance your own projects without investors.

Be on the lookout for fake supporters who may have ulterior motives. People will seek to be your friend because they want something from you. They will try to benefit off you for their own personal gain. Others may be completely supportive to your face, but be hating on you behind your back. Be prepared to hold your ground and move forward with or without a team behind you.

"Cowards die many times before their actual deaths."

— Julius Caesar

BAD BYTCH RULE NO. 30: There is two types of women in this world. One type hustles and gets out there and gets it, while them other bytchez just sit at home talking shyt about us.

"End of the story I followed the code, cracked the safe....other n*ggas aint in da game so they practice hate" — Jay-Z

Life is not a spectator sport. You can either jump out there and get in the game or you will be stuck at the sidelines making useless commentary. Which would you rather be? The one whom is out there really living and really taking chances or would you rather be the one sitting at home talking shyt, but never getting off the couch. You decide.

You may not win them all. You may not always walk away with the prize. The point is that you got off you're a$$ and got in the game. Some opportunities are more about the experience, not the outcome. The important thing to do is keep trying. Stay busy and keep give these hoes something to talk about.

"Throughout life people will make you mad, disrespect you and treat you bad. Let God deal with the things they do, cause hate in your heart will consume you too. " – Will Smith

BAD BYTCH RULE NO. 31: Never apologize or take blame for something that you did not do. Of course, admit to your mistakes, but never no one else's!!

"The most common way people give up their power is by thinking they don't have any."

— Alice Walker

Everyone loves a scapegoat. As bad as it is to have a scapegoat, it is even worse to be one. Never let someone attribute a mistake to you that you did not make. Utilize your power to nip that shyt right in the bud. Of course, you should admit to your own mistakes and learn from them. It takes a real woman to own up and admit when they are wrong. **However, it would take a complete idiot to allow someone to blame their problems on you.**

Keep your foot down and let muthafukkas know that you only take credit when credit is due. To make a mistake is human and you can learn from it. There is nothing to learn from a mistake that you did not make. Make muthafukkas accountable for their own bad judgments.

"Nothing is more intolerable than to have to admit to yourself your own errors."

— Ludwig van Beethoven

BAD BYTCH RULE NO. 32: **Never run from your problems. Always run towards them. Address them and handle them quickly and discreetly. Keep private matters private.**

"I am willing to put myself through anything, temporary pain or discomfort means nothing to me as long as I can see that the experience will take me to a new level. I am interested in the unknown, and the only path to the unknown is through breaking barriers, an often painful process."

– Diana Nyad

Learn to meet all conditions head on with no avoidance. When a problem arises handle it immediately. Find practical ways to deal with life situations. Address all issues early on, before they have the opportunity to bubble over into a more serious situation. Grown women do not run from their problems. There is no room in a boss's lifestyle for **fear** or **worry**. Those are negative emotions that do nothing for you. Why worry when you can pray?

First step is to handling an issue is to acknowledge it exists. Once you're able to admit to your problems, immediately take steps to resolve any issue with positivity. Look for the absolute best solution and implement it as soon as possible. Control the outcome to the very best of your ability.

Learn to be as discreet as possible. You do not want your resolutions to be water downed by unneeded opinions and advice. Always keep your personal issues off social networks for the world to see. Why should your personal problems ever become a public debate? That's just begging other people to judge you and talk shyt to you and about you. **Overly emotional tweets and facebook status's are for suckas.** After you resolve your issues and are no longer thinking about it them, you will always have people still judging you of them if you play them out in public. Make sure to only put out there, what you want to be known for.

The problems may take your focus for a moment and demand some time and attention; however they become tiny when you compare them to all the amazing things a Bad Bytch is able to accomplish.

"Either pray or worry, but don't do both."

– 50 Cents

BAD BYTCH RULE NO. 33: **Boss Bytchez make strong, intelligent, concrete decisions and stand firmly by them. Never use term "I don't know."**

"I am so territorial, that [from the start] I just felt like whatever I was gonna do I was gonna write it myself, its my personal preference to always be in control of everything I do in life." – Nicki Minaj

You have to know what you want out of life. **You have to be able to voice your opinion in a way that is firm and believable.** There is no getting around that. These muthafukkas are like kids. If they don't hear in your voice that you are serious, they won't take you seriously. Never show signs of weakness.

If you don't know the answer to something or haven't decided what you want, very simply explain to the other party that you need some time to weigh out your options and make a concrete decision. You have to believe in your ability to make intelligent decisions which are in the best interest of you, your family and your career.

Take any time that you need to research and make a strong choice. Stand by your choices and decisions even if it means you're the only one standing there. Trust your ability to choose correctly.

Anything that you accomplish through your own choices and ideas are truly yours. You can proud of seeing your dreams and ideas come to life. Be happy you have been able to make strong decisions and take delight that this ability can never be taken from you. Stay Bossy!

"The most courageous act is still to think for yourself. Aloud."

— Coco Chanel

BAD BYTCH RULE NO. 34: If there is something good happening in your today in your life, you have got to go with it immediately. No hesitations, No excuses!

"The world is given to you as a beautiful garden. You diminish the garden if you do not enjoy the fruits."

—Mother Theresa

Success comes from being properly prepared to take advantage of every opportunity that life presents to you. Some opportunities may be more inconvenient than others. **You must leave your comfort zone or opportunities will be lost.** Maintain a positive attitude and be prepared to do whatever it takes to achieve your goals.

Never put anything off that can be done today. Never make up excuses why you aren't getting it done. Just work really hard, get it done and let the hoes hate you for it.

"I love to see a young girl go out and grab the world by the lapels. Life's a bytch. You've got to go out and kick ass."

– Maya Angelou

BAD BYTCH RULE NO. 35: There is a time to work, a time to play, and a time to rest. Know the difference. When its time to work, keep it professional.

"The most effective way to do it, is to do it."

- Amelia Earhart

Time management is such an underrated skill. Any successful person will tell you that you have to keep your schedule together. Have certain hours of the day that you set aside for working or studying. That way you can catch yourself if you start slipping and get off schedule.

Track your time for a week and see how much of your time you are wasting. Know how many hours a week you watch television. How many hours are you spending on your phone, on your computer, and on social networks? **Time is truly money. Get all your important business taken care of prior to participating in leisure activities.** Allow yourself time to relax and rest, but limit that time to a reasonable amount. Trade in stationary activities for more productive ones such as exercise.

When you know it is time to work, then be professional and get the work done proficiently. Keep your emotions out of a business setting. A workplace is not appropriate for emotional outburst. Check the bullshyt in at the door. **Never play around or sleep around where you make your money at.**

"Great leaders are almost always great simplifiers, who can cut through argument, debate and doubt, to offer a solution everybody can understand."

 – *Colin Powell*

BAD BYTCH RULE NO. 36: Rather then argue with a stupid bytch, turn them in to a fan, resolve the issue with positivity and gain a loyal fan.

"Dearly beloved, avenge not yourselves, but rather give place unto wrath: for it is written, Vengeance is mine; I will repay, saith the Lord. Be not overcome of evil, but overcome evil with good."
—Romans 12:19, 21

Argue with a stupid bytch and someone watching from a distance may not be able to tell who is who. Women developing at a beginner's level may simply not be able to comprehend your reasoning. Their intellect and maturity level just can't comprehend a Bad Bytch's policies. Arguing with them is a waste of your time and energy. You will never achieve anything through fussing and arguing with them. Common ground will be impossible.

Instead, just flip the game on them and turn on the natural Bad Bytch charm. Quickly resolve the issue with a positive attitude and stay humble. It's all about Public Relations at the end of the day. That's why celebrities always take the higher road out of situations and do damage control.

Before you allow someone to take you up out your character, take them up out your atmosphere. Wash your hands of negative situations and allow God to handle them.

"Arguments will seldom change the aspects or the views of any. And truth needs no champion, for it is of itself champion of champions — and needs no defense; only for self to live according to that which IS the truth."

— Edgar Cayce

BAD BYTCH RULE NO. 37: Never ever get to close to a woman identified as a zombie hoe. A zombie hoe has no brains and moves to damn slow.

"When you look at the dark side, careful you must be ... for the dark side looks back."
-Yoda

This one is a no brainer (pun intended). You are the company that you keep. Examine your inner circle very wisely. Why would you want to get caught up with the hoe that falls down in all the scary movies and gets up getting caught? I'd much rather be with the female that will stop, drop, roll, duck and shoot back with me.

Women developing at a beginner's level tend to move to slowly. Always hesitating and shyt. Spend your time with people whom can match your speed and reaction time. A Bad Bytch is known for making quick, intelligent decisions. Keep only boss's in your inner circle that can easily match you with speed and wit. The wrong female companions can slow you down.

"Nevertheless the passions, whether violent or not, should never be so expressed as to reach the point of causing disgust; and music, even in situations of the greatest horror, should never be painful to the ear but should flatter and charm it, and thereby always remain music." - Mozart

BAD BYTCH RULE NO. 38: When MONEY calls, it calls. No complaining about hard work or a little sleep. Find the strength and motivation to make it.

"This is my plan. When I'm in the studio making a hit record, I'm not trying to make a hit record; I'm making one. This is what I studied. This is why I stay up twenty hours a day."

— Sean Diddy Combs

No one ever promised you that it would be easy. Have you ever heard the saying "If you want something done, ask a busy person to do it." If it is something that makes sense or could help out with their position in life, a busy person will find a way to get it done. People with exuberant amounts of free time also tend to have exuberant amounts of excuses why they can't do it.

The hustle is the best part of the game. Be prepared to work very hard, very long hours. Success requires a tremendous amount of dedication. The wealthy are not wealthy from sitting on their a$$. The sitting on the a$$ probably didn't even start until they were completely financially secure.

Your mind will tire before your body and tell you that you cannot go on when physically you can. **Push yourself very hard every single day to make accomplishments and know that all your hard work will pay off in the end.**

"When I started flirtin with the hustle, failure became my ex. Now I'm engaged to the game and married to success. "

-Lil Wayne

BAD BYTCH RULE NO. 39: **You will never be truly successful until you learn to congratulate and take joy in someone else's success.**

"The people that are inclined to hate are also inclined to be losers. A loser could never congratulate a winner — it's not in them."

— Nicki Minaj

In God's eyes, we are all sisters, just developing on different levels during our experience here on earth. **If one of your sisters achieves high levels of success, it will open up many doors for you.** I can write this book today because several of my sisters that came along before me fought for women's rights and freedom of speech. They wrote quality books that made publishers take chances on young minority women. I congratulate them on their success, because they paved the way it what will lead to my success.

Someone else's success does not mean your downfall. Celebrate for your sister and share in her joy and positive energy. They are experiencing success because they have worked very hard for it. Let it motivate you to do better yourself.

"You can't speak on other peoples blessing because you don't know what they had to go through to deserve those blessings." — Blac Chyna

BAD BYTCH RULE NO. 40: The silliest bytch of them all, is the one whom is sucking and fucking everyone and is still uneducated and broke.

"In Hollywood they say there's no business like show business. In the hood they say there's no business like ho' business." – 50 Cents

Pu$$y is Power. Some of our sisters must have missed the memo. Maybe they didn't get to heard any of Beyoncé's music. Who runs this world? Women do! **Respect and Love yourself. Value your pu$$y. Not as in prostitution, but in self value.**

A true Bad Bytch will get plenty attention from males with never even sleeping with them. We can run pockets without even given up the pu$$y. We could, not that we do. We work hard through life; you have the right not to fuck with lames. Value yourself and your time. Don't allow the people you deal with intimately waste your time.

Ladies, if you thinks it's possible that you are a side chick or hoe, ask your selves the following questions. Does this man have any interest in your goals and dreams in life? If the answer is no, then what the fuck you fuckin with him for? Does he take you out in public? Does he celebrate Holidays and Birthdays with you? Does he even know your real name? Or better yet do you even know is? Does he spend time getting to know you? Have you been to his house? Does he know your favorite color or your favorite food? Does he even care about that? Does he know what your childhood was like? Have you met his family, close friends or children? Come on now ladies, we really got to smarten up. **If your answer is No to one or more of those questions, ding ding ding, You're quite possibly a Hoe!**

As long as you let men run through you, they will run through you. The little effort they put in, means you will have very little to show for it. When women give it up to easily, they will literally walk away with nothing but a bad reputation.

Fellow Bad Bytchez, consider yourself warned. Be very afraid of these lost and confused young women. Is it not bad enough to be a hoe? Nowadays, these hoes are also uneducated and broke. They are getting absolutely nothing out the deal. They will try to corrupt your life with their whorish ways. Avoid them like the plague.

I understand there are some women may just really enjoy sex. It is fine to be a freak and love sex. Just be sure to handle yourself with respect. How about pick out a dick and stick to it. Protect yourself at all times. Always take time to handle your own business.

You have to set the standard for how people are going to treat you in life. Love and respect yourself so others will treat you with love and respect also. Men always recognize the women who handle their business. They will show them more respect because they know that we make our own money, are educated and working hard to further our success in life.

Avoid women whose entire focus is off. Men will treat them according to their whorish ways. Their whoring will turn into a form of self-mutilation. Their pu$$y will suffer. Avoid this female at all costs she is on a downward spiral and may attempt to pull you down with her.

"If you want love, then faithfully, practice living the principles of love....work on yourself and no one else."
—Marilyn Monroe

BAD BYTCH RULE NO. 41: Its not enough to claim a belief in certain ideals, but you must consistently live as such. Don't be a hypocrite.

"....Man shall not live by bread alone, but by every word that proceedeth out of the mouth of God." – Matthew 4:4

It is very easy to say what you would never do. Until experience a certain situation, it's hard to say exactly what you would do. If you are going to make it a mission in your life to claim a belief whether it is spiritual or political make sure you are prepared to live up to it.

Don't preach against abortion, then when you experience an unwanted pregnancy, the first thing you do is run to go get an abortion. Don't badmouth gays and then proposition someone in a bathroom. **If you are going to state claims in certain ideals make sure your life is consistent with those ideals. Hypocrisy is for the weak minded. Make sure you know what you believe in. Be prepared to back up every single claim you make with your actions.**

"When someone shows you who they are, believe them the first time."
– Maya Angelou

BAD BYTCH RULE NO. 42: **Some women will claim that they want success, but never aggressively pursue it. Your attitude and motivation plays the biggest factor in your own success.**

"But I can say that life is good to me. Has been and is good. So I think my task is to be good to it. So how do you be good to life? You live it."

— Morgan Freeman

In life, most people are about as happy as they want to be. They are successful as they chose to be. We live in a world where everyone who publicly claims to be CEO's never even owned their own company. The will claim to be a boss of their own company, but never made a pay roll before.

Everyone wants to try and convince you that they are rich and famous, yet never want to put the work in behind it. Are they really trying to convince you, or are they trying to convince themselves too? You cannot build a business on a shoe string unless you are building a shoestring business.

Without a well thought out, clear and concise plan, a goal is just a dream. You have to have the motivation to get behind it and work hard every single day to achieve it. Your attitude is the absolute biggest factor in your own success. If you chose to have an attitude that you will only do what's convenient, then you will not go very far. If you expect others to do the work for you, then you are destined to fail. If you have a positive attitude that you will do whatever it takes to achieve your goals, you are an unstoppable force!

Networking with other women is a beautiful and wonderful thing. Just be sure that the women you team up with are actually making moves and are not just all talk.

"Visualize this thing that you want, see it, feel it, believe in it. Make your mental blue print, and begin to build."
— Robert Collier

BAD BYTCH RULE NO. 43: Grown women don't gossip nor spread rumors about each other. Leave that for the basic bytchez to do. Because quite frankly if it's not effecting our money or our family, we just don't give a fuck.

"Great minds discuss ideas, average minds discuss events, small minds discuss people."

– Eleanor Roosevelt.

Compassion is such an underrated trait. **When rumors are spread it can be hurtful to the person it is about.** Half the damn time the rumors aren't even true. **Believe none of what you hear and only about half of what you see.** Half of this shyt is an illusion and people make you see what they want you to. The game is cutthroat. People will lie and spread malicious rumors about someone else for no damn reason at all.

Leave the high school games for the high schoolers. We are grown women over here. Never repeat negativity that you hear about one of your sisters. Its hurtful and a waste of time. It will expend negative karma from you that you will have to face later. If the rumors or the person they are about do not have a direct impact on your financial matters or on your family let the bullshyt go in one ear and out the damn other.

If you are a Bad Bytch who is having an issue with people spreading rumors about you, I suggest you adopt a typical "kiss my ass" type attitude. Give an official statement that you would like to tell whomever is out there talking shyt to kiss your muthafukkin ass on a sunny day.

Don't be penetrated by the negativity and bullshyt that people will through your way. **You do not owe anybody an explanation for anything. Only seek out God's approval in life.** Anyone else's opinions, rumors or fabricated stories can fall to the side. Only address a situation if it comes from higher up than you. That way you can defeat the offender and take their energy and fan base.

"When I see your name on Billboard, then I'll respond to you. If you are bitter, get a life! You're gonna go down in history as a sore loser instead of the Queen. If you can't beat 'em, join 'em. Don't play with me. When I see it on the Billboard, that's when I'll respond."

— Nicki Minaj

BAD BYTCH RULE NO. 44: Never feel ashamed of where you came from. Never feel ashamed of what you have been through. The greatest leaders have emerged from the most humble beginnings.

I was raised by a single mother who made a way for me. She used to scrub floors as a domestic worker, put a cleaning rag in her pocketbook and ride the subways in Brooklyn so I would have food on the table. But she taught me as I walked her to the subway that life is about not where you start, but where you're going."

— Reverend Al Sharpton

Pick any child right now out of the hoodest of all the hoods. Teach him the proper mentality, attitude and motivation. He will be able to become the next greatest leader, regardless of where he is from. **It is possible to be in your surroundings, but not OF your surroundings. It is never about where you are at or where you are from. It is always about where you are going.**

You can shut your muthafukkin door and run your household any way that you want. **It does not cost anything to raise your kids in a household filled with love and respect. Who's to say children from the hood shouldn't get to listen to Wolfgang Amadeus**

Mozart or Ludwig van Beethoven. **Show them the work of Picasso. Read them every children's book that won a Caldecott Medal from the American Library Association. Teach them that they can be anything that they set their minds to. Encourage them to set their aim very high!** These are advantages in life that you can provide for your children at little or no cost to you.

If you yourself have experienced a traumatic childhood or any traumatic events in your life, never feel ashamed about it. **Derive strength from the experience. Refuse to keep being a victim. Start healing yourself immediately. Start educating yourself immediately.**

There is absolutely no doubt that you could start off scrubbing toilets and end up owning the whole company. **Believe in yourself. You can achieve any goal that you set your mind to.** Have special ways to keep your self-focused. Enlighten yourself. Dare to reach higher mentalities. **Use the arts, reading, and music to help you escape your atmosphere into a more creative one.** It is perfectly fine to have a great variety of influences in your life. Some of your influences may be street, gritty, hustle-hard type shyt. Some may be playful compositions. Some may be deep , intricate beautiful masterpieces. Never limit yourself to just one genre of anything. Stay focused and stay learning. Learn from a variety of teachers in a variety of subjects. Your possibilities are infinite.

"Music is the one incorporeal entrance into the higher world of knowledge which comprehends mankind but which mankind cannot comprehend." – Ludwig van Beethoven

BAD BYTCH RULE NO. 45: When someone tries to discourage you, and believe me they will, don't ever believe in them, believe in yourself.

"To acquire true self power you have to feel beneath no one, be immune to criticism and be fearless."

— Deepak Chopra

You have made it to a point where you have set goals for yourself. You are working hard every day to achieve them. Not everyone is going to be a supporter for you. There are many who may try to discourage you. The naysayers are all around. It may surprise you where the negativity begins to come from.

There will be friends, co-workers, loved ones, or even family members who will try to talk you out of pursuing your dreams. They will approach you with their fears and a list of cons, rather than pros. It hurts when those closest to you cannot see your vision with you. You may have even trusted these naysayers in the past with their advice. Then when it comes to your vision in life they cannot say anything positive. I know it hurts. That's my reasoning for creating The Bad Bytch Support Network.

When people try to discourage you from pursuing your dreams, they are expressing their fears to you. Make sure you understand that those are simply their fears and not yours. Don't allow anyone to beat your ears up with negative nonsense. **Even if someone does not understand your goals, they should respect them**. If you listen to the naysayers you will miss out on valuable experiences and opportunities. You don't want to be wondering later on in life what would of the outcome be had you pursued your dreams anyway. Continue on your mission and let them live their live a life full of regret.

To stay focused, utilize prayer. Spend time in solitude, where it's just you, God and your dreams. Seek out God's approval on your life decisions. Everyone else's opinion can just fall to the side. **With God on your side no one can be against you.** Believe in yourself! Believe in your dreams! Believe in the promises He has made to you! Pursue your goals, full throttle, despite anyone whom doesn't like it.

"Ever since we were little, we were so on fire for our dreams. We never let anyone blow our flames out."

- Kelly Rowland

<u>BAD BYTCH RULE NO. 46</u>: Some "No's" are really "Yes's" in disguise. A stern "No" may really mean to re-group and try again. Come harder and come stronger next time.

"We may encounter many defeats but we must not be defeated."

– Maya Angelou

Life is full of Yes's and No's. Sometimes the answer you get will be in your favor. That will make it a lot easier to proceed. However, be prepared that sometimes in life you will hear the words "No".

When you hear this word, immediately switch it in your mind to "not right now". Accept that "No" is simply the answer for now. Make sure you understand why you are being told "No" right now. You may have to re-group. Identify what is missing and how you landed at a less desired outcome. Do you need more paperwork? Were your items incomplete or not in order? Did you need prior approval, more certifications?!? Find out exactly what the issue was, accept it and work to correct things.

Take an adequate amount of time to re-plan and try again. Ensure that this time you come back stronger and harder than before. Pay more attention to the finer details. Create a greater likelihood of a more favorable result.

Keep trying and try again until you achieve your goal. Allow any discouragement felt to be short lived and pass quickly into the rebuilding stages. Carefully flip all your negatives into positives to get the answer that you want.

"Negative results are just what I want. They're just as valuable to me as positive results. I can never find the thing that does the job best until I find the ones that don't."

—Thomas Edison

BAD BYTCH RULE NO. 47: People will purposely confuse you and lead you the wrong way. When looking for advice, go with in and trust your own instincts.

"And uh, my real friends never hearin' from me

Fake friends write the wrong answers on the mirror for me

That's why I pick and choose, I don't get shyt confused

I got a small circle, I'm not with different crews

We walk the same path, but got on different shoes

Live in the same building, but we got different views"

– Drake

People have been coveting information since before the great pyramids of Egypt were built. Some may be fearful that you will live up to your full potential and become a fierce competitor. Others still operate under the policies that your success could somehow equal their downfall. Drake said it best. "Fake friends will write the wrong answer on the mirror for you" So when you look at your reflection you see the wrong answers.

Take all advice with a grain of salt. Forgive those that purposely mislead you, because they do it out of fear and jealously. They may purposely mislead you or hide information from you that could be beneficial to your development.

Genuine and trustworthy advisors are rare. When you are in need of advice, meditate. Learn how to quiet your mind and go within yourself. **Ask God for guidance. Listen to your intuition. Your intuition is really your Angels speaking to you and bringing you answers from God.** Learn how to quiet your mind enough that you can hear them clearly.

"Fake hoes give real bytchez a bad a name."

— Tyga Quotes

BAD BYTCH RULE NO. 48: A smart business woman knows never to let any portion of her career totally depend on what another person is going to do. Stay in control at all times.

"Few are those who see with their own eyes and feel with their own hearts."

— Albert Einstein

Accept full responsibility for your own future. You decide what you want to achieve in life and it is your responsibility to make your dreams a reality. Keep the ball in your court at all times. You must stay in control.

Learn how to delegate minimal tasks effectively. Delegation is a part of being a boss, but you must learn to never rely totally on someone else. Only delegate tasks to people whom you know through experience can handle it correctly. Only delegate tasks that you can quickly recover from if handled inappropriately.

Your career should never depend totally on the choices that someone else makes. Then you are no longer in control. Your success will depend on that person. **You can never truly expect someone to get out here and make things happen for you more than you can yourself.**

"You cannot always control what goes on outside. But you can always control what goes on inside."

— Wayne Dyer

<u>BAD BYTCH RULE NO. 49</u>: Never sleep on a Bad Bytch. When you finally wake up, we will be at the top waving and laughing.

"Some people say I have attitude--maybe I do...But I think you have to. You have to believe in yourself when no one else does--that makes you a winner right there."

—Venus Williams

If someone underestimates your life potential may God bless them. You may have done everything you can to explain to others your future plans and ask for support. People may or may not believe in you. They may miss out on some awesome business opportunities.

If they miss out, then they miss out. You will be at the top waving at them before you know it. **Results will convert all non-believers to believers.**

"Champions aren't made in the gyms. Champions are made from something they have deep inside them -- a desire, a dream, a vision."

- Muhammad Ali

BAD BYTCH RULE NO. 50: A true Bad Bytch is like the Postman. No matter rain, sleet or snow, we are up, ready and on our muthafukkin job.

"A dream doesn't become reality through magic; it takes sweat, determination and hard work."

– Colin Powell

Ensure that your work ethics are impeccable. To reach success you have to want it more than the next bytch. You have to be willing to go above and beyond. You have to show up early and work later. You have to be up and working when your competition is sleeping. This effort has to be expended from you.

Be reliable! When you have somewhere to be, show up when you say you are going to. When you give someone your word, you **must** follow through with it.

There may be people whom are relying on you to be there. Your children are depending on you for their well- being. No matter the weather, no matter what you are going through, no matter how little sleep you had, you have to be up and ready to work. Be willing to put forth the extra effort to make it to the top.

"We often miss opportunity, because it's dressed in overalls and looks like work."

–Thomas Edison

BAD BYTCH RULE NO. 51: Its always a Bad Bytchez job to
ballerina these hoes. You know, keep them on their tippy toes.

"Models now need to promote themselves, think like businesswomen and diversify their careers by doing other things. Chances are very slim that a mere model will become a household name today."

—Tyra Banks

Stay one up on the competition at all times. Normally, this can be accomplished simply by being your own unique self. Keep a style which is unique to you. If the entire crowd is going left field, then hang a right on their a$$e$. **Keep people guessing on what your next move is going to be.**

Build a portfolio which is very diverse. **You never have to be just one thing. A Bad Bytch is capable wearing very many hats**. You are capable of having many successful careers at one time. Feel free to step out your comfort zone and venture out into unfamiliar territory.

Take yourself and your business very seriously. Work very hard to stay winning. If what you are doing is inspiring others and keeping them on top their game then you are a natural born leader and a Bad Bytch indeed.

"Do you really want to look back on your life and see how wonderful it could have been had you not been afraid to live it?"
– Caroline Myss

BAD BYTCH RULE NO. 52: Only clowns jump through hoops. Recognize bullshyt when you see it, then immediately denounce it.

"These bytchez ain't real, they just real clown bytchez
I remember when they used to feel like real down bytchez
I'm from a city where respect don't come from currency
And I don't wanna hear what you gonna do, what you done currently"
— Lola Monroe

Rebuke bullshyt away from you just like you would rebuke the devil. In business settings and in the entertainment industry you will get people that will make astronomic promises to you of how they can make you a star or make you successful. Of course they can, all you have to do is pay them your hard earned money, work for free or stand on one foot and bark like a muthafukkin dog. Recognize a bullshyter when you see one. Life is too short for the bullshyt.

There are some scam artist out there who base their entire existence on scheming on people who have goals and dreams. It's unfortunate that they prey on people that are out here trying to accomplish something good with their life.

Don't fall for no bullshyters. Do your homework on everyone who is wanting to work with you. Especially if they are charging a fee for their services. If there is too many unclear answers and bullshyt in the fine print, don't be afraid to tell them thanks, but no thanks.

"The deadliest bullshyt is odorless and transparent."

– William Gibson

BAD BYTCH RULE NO. 53: Laugh at people whom consider you competition and only compete with your previous years financial records.

"I came, I saw, I conquered." — Julius Caesar

There is nothing wrong with a little friendly competition with your colleagues. It will help you improve on the quality and presentation of your work. However, there is some that take the friendly competition thing a little too far.

Competition can get uglier than the political ads at election time. Learn to brush off negativity with laughter. Women developing at a beginner's level do not understand that only 4% of the population controls over 96% of the world's money. That means there is enough money to take and everyone to eat. Their reaction is out of fear, that if you make it, somehow they won't. **The moment that friendly competition turns negative, brush your shoulders off and only compete with yourself.**

Pull out your financial records from the previous year and make sure that this year you top that. Start looking at bigger houses, work on earning another degree, challenge yourself to go further in life each year then what you did the previous year.

A warning to those whom are seeking success on a national level: Continuously competing at the local level can keep you local. Seek out the Masters whom have reached either national or global success. That is whom you have to inspire to surpass.

"Please you can never compare to me, all these bytchez is scared of me, I am who they couldn't even dare to be!"

— Nicki Minaj

BAD BYTCH RULE NO. 54: Life is a game of chess. The Queen is the strongest player on the chess board. Now maneuver ladies and protect your thrown.

"All men can see these tactics whereby I conquer, but what none can see is the strategy out of which victory is evolved."

—Sun Tzu

We can learn a lot from a chess game. In order to win, you have to plan and strategize. Learn and understand all the key players on your team and how to use them most effectively. Now take those same rules and apply them to life. We are the Queens. The absolute strongest player, who can make the most maneuvers. We have to command our army. Life has to be planned and well thought out to achieve success.

Utilize everything in your arsenal to better your position in life. Always look for areas of weakness. Never leave yourself open to be vulnerable. The enemy is always lurking for ways to take you down. Keep your eyes wide open ladies and protect your thrown.

"Leaders establish the vision for the future and set the strategy for getting there; they cause change. They motivate and inspire others to go in the right direction and they, along with everyone else, sacrifice to get there." — John Kotter

BAD BYTCH RULE NO. 55: Never bite the hand that feeds you. If someone is legitimately a positive force in your life, they deserve your Trust, Love and Loyalty.

"I think we deserve people who really, really love us."

— Alicia Keys

Throughout your life you will know hundreds and hundreds of people. Just a handful of those people will be help-mate. A help-mate is someone whom truly has your best interest in mind. They will be a positive and motivating influence in your life. When you are blessed enough to have this person in your life, make sure you treat them with love and gratitude.

Be very aware of your karma and your energy. If you were to cross someone whom is good to you, the karma you would receive in return will totally kick you're a$$. All those who love you are beautiful. Hurting someone who loves you, is a form of self-abuse. Learn to have appreciation and show gratitude to the ones that deserve it.

"I just don't know how to deal with so many people giving me that much affection. I never had that in my life."

— Tupac Shakur

BAD BYTCH RULE NO. 56: Don't allow the Government to define what "The American Dream" is to you. Own your dreams and write your own path!

"I am the American Dream. I am the epitome of what the American Dream basically said. It said, you could come from anywhere and be anything you want in this country. That's exactly what I've done."

—Whoopi Goldberg

When you are making your plans for your life, don't be afraid to think out of the box. Do not become brainwashed by society standards of what the American Dream is. Your dream may not be the white picket fence and 2.5 children. For many that is a very happy life, but you my fellow Bad Bytch may crave something more than the typical. Feel free to write out your own dream and make society conform to you.

The government would like you to believe that The American Dream is graduating high school, going to college, taking out student loans, buying a house and a car, then working the rest of your life to pay off your debt. Re-write that into a better way to fits your preference.

God has given us free-will, which makes our life's possibilities absolutely infinite. "Fear not, for I am with thee" should be on your heart at all times.

Education should be a large part of your life from start to finish. Not just being educated in the classroom, but also in world experience. If you can benefit from traveling to other countries or moving to a different state, don't be afraid to try it. Provide yourself a proper environment for your spirit to live in.

Research out paths which are less traveled or make your own path. The majority of self-made millionaires in the United States are people whom started their own business. Meditate and reach within yourself to decide what is best for you and your life. You write your own "American Dream".

"Education is transformational. It changes lives. That is why people work so hard to become educated and why education has always been the key to the American Dream, the force that erases arbitrary divisions of race and class and culture and unlocks every person's God-given potential."
— Condoleezza Rice

BAD BYTCH RULE NO. 57: Bad Bytch on the Streetz, Boss Bytch in the board room, Porn star in the bedroom.

"This is for the time you gave me flowers
For the world that is ours
For the mula, for the power of love
And no I won't never ever e-ever give you up
And I wanna say thank you in case I don't thank you enough
A woman in the street and a freak in the you know what
Sit back, sit back, it's the pre-game show
Daddy you know what's up!"
– Beyoncé

In public you are a certified Bad Bytch. In business you are sharp, intellectual and well-respected. Close that bedroom door and we have a totally different woman. Maybe even a whole new ultra ego comes out. Just like how Beyonce has Sasha Fierce, we have the right to let go all inhibitions in the bedroom.

Once you have decided on a deserving and appropriate partner, make it your business to discover exactly what turns them on in the bedroom. I think all men have a secret fetish. Something that just drives them absolutely crazy in the bedroom. Once you find out what your partner can't resist, learn how to do it well and do it often.

Be a firm believer in the power of the pu$$y to tame and control your significant other. Be sexy, be daring, be romantic, be freaky, whatever you do just have fun with it and enjoy yourself!

"Guys wanna wife me 'n' give me the ring I'll do it anywhere, anyhow, down for anything."

— Lil Kim

BAD BYTCH RULE NO. 58: Your wish is Your command. Choose exactly what you want in life and pursue it aggressively and persistently.

"I have noticed even people who claim everything is predestined, and that we can do nothing to change it, look before they cross the road."

— Stephen Hawking

The power to change your life for the best resides within you.
There is so much to be obtained from the right mental attitude. Take responsibility for your life and for your situations. **Live your life for a purpose greater than yourself.**

Begin with feeling grateful for what you already have. When you express gratitude for what you are already blessed with, you are opening up the doors to receive more blessings.

Next, set an ideal for your life. An ideal is a spiritual ideal of what you envision your best life possible to be. Know exactly what you want out of life and establish the right purposes for it.

Take complete charge of your future. Create short term reachable goals and long terms goals that take more time and effort. Work like thunder every single day to achieve and journal your progress. Stay focused and don't let anyone or anything deter you from your plan.

"Be thankful for what you have; you'll end up having more. If you concentrate on what you don't have, you will never, ever have enough."

— Oprah Winfrey

BAD BYTCH RULE NO. 59: Pick and choose your battles very wisely. Only fight righteous battles, which deserve your time, money and attention.

"The general who wins the battle makes many calculations in his temple before the battle is fought. The general who loses makes but few calculations beforehand."

- Sun Tzu

Anger when used correctly can serve a good purpose. A person with no temper is indeed a very weak person. A person who cannot control their temper is much much much worse. When someone is infringing on the divine purpose of your life, then a righteous wraith may emerge. The struggle, the combat and the victory can be beautiful. A Bad Bytch may be forced to be a warrior. However, you have to carefully choose your enemies and your battles so they are not destructive to you.

First, examine the reason of conflict. Decide if what you are fighting for is righteous. Or is it simply due to you attempting to gratify selfish desires? Correspond your reaction correctly.

War can both destroy and create. It can be counter-productive and explosive. Think before you react in fiery. Learn to channel your anger in the appropriate direction. It is natural to feel furious, but allow that fury motivate you to do something positive to change things.

"I don't oppose all wars. What I am opposed to is a dumb war. What I am opposed to is a rash war."

—President Barack Obama

BAD BYTCH RULE NO. 60: Never waste time trying to reason with someone whom is unreasonable. It's like banging your head into a wall. Pointless.

"Muthafukkas say that I'm foolish I only talk about jewels/ Do you fools listen to music or do you just skim through it?/ See I'm influenced by the ghetto you ruined / That same dude you gave nothing, I made something doing"

— Jay Z

We will come across some people in life who believe that they are more important to others. They have distorted images of reality and distorted images of themselves. This comes from a lack of understanding of logic and truth. Their level of development is too basic to even begin reasoning with them.

They are simply not at a level of mentality where they can comprehend what you are saying. You can explain it over and over and they just don't understand. It will take them being educated and having more real life experience to be able to wrap their minds the voice of reason.

If you try a couple times and the truth seems to just keep flying right over their head, just agree to disagree and move on. Your time is too valuable to waste it on someone whom is being unreasonable.

"It is impossible for a man to learn what he thinks he already knows."

—Epictetus

BAD BYTCH RULE NO. 61: **The very exact moment that you notice someone is wasting your time, immediately and abruptly cut them off. Life is too short for any bullshyt.**

"Some people make your life better by walking into it while other people make your life better by simply walking out of it." - Wiz Khalifa

Anything born of falsehoods and bullshyt is destined to pass away. Bullshyters are destructive. Their lies and manipulation are destructive to the mind and the physical body.

Never get yourself caught up in imagined circumstances. Make people value your time and efforts. The moment that you notice someone is wasting your time; excuse them immediately from your life. Spend your time with people whom are genuine and motivating.

"Look, if you had one shot, or one opportunity

To seize everything you ever wanted in one moment

Would you capture it or just let it slip?"

–Eminem

BAD BYTCH RULE NO. 62: **Always identify the players on your team's strong points and weak points. Utilize each to the best of their abilities.**

"I tell people all the time, 'You want to work for me? You have to give 250,000%,' because when I'm in the booth, I don't half-ass it. I demand perfection from everyone around me and if you can't live up to that, then bye-bye."

— Nicki Minaj

Know your inner circle and know it well. Examine each person whom plays a significant role in your life. Know their strong points and their weak points. Know what you can depend on them for and what you cant.

Identify who the weakest player is on your team. You can either try to strengthen the weakest player or decide to pull their extra weight. If it becomes too much for you to handle, then you must change the conditions around you. Re-structure your crew and severe ties with the weak players.

Ensure that everyone on your team knows their position and is comfortable with it. Stimulate your team to be focused and productive. Without clarity, focus and harmony there can be no gain, just confusion. A small group of people whom all focused on the same positive purpose can accomplish much in life.

"I will always choose a lazy person to do a difficult job because, definitely he will find an easy way to do that"

– Bill Gates

BAD BYTCH RULE NO. 63: **Not everyone belongs within your inner circle. Pick and choose your close associates wisely. Always verify their backgrounds and their resume.**

"Some will hate you, pretend they love you, then behind your back try to eliminate you, but who Jah bless no man curse."

—Bob Marley

It is always fun to be sociable and meet new people. With technology and social networking nowadays, you have the ability to connect with people in other cities, states even countries. This can be a good and positive thing or it can turn negative pretty quickly. Now, people now have access to your personal information, your personal pictures, your likes and your dislikes.

You may meet someone and seem like you have a lot in common, but it could be because they have done their homework on you. Remember, live in a world where you can believe none of what you hear and only half of what we see. It is okay to be friendly, but be very, very picky about whom you allow in your inner circle.

Watch that your inner circle does not be overcome with false characters and faked relationships. Make sure to verify people's background and their claims before you allow them into your personal life.

"Et tu, Brute"

— Shakespeare's Julius Caesar

BAD BYTCH RULE NO. 64: The absolute biggest factor in your own success is your ATTITUDE! Don't be ashamed to admit when you need an attitude adjustment. Simply adjust your attitude quickly and discreetly.

"Life Is About Moving On, Accepting Changes And Looking Forward To What Makes You Stronger And More Complete..."

— Q Owner of World Star

Be thankful and appreciative for everything you do have. In your possession right now today, you have all the resources needed to build a better tomorrow. **Give glory to God for what you do have, and you will be undoubtly blessed with more**.

You can rid yourself of a bad attitude through positive thinking techniques. Track your feelings and figure out where the negative thoughts and patterns are deriving from. Release any negative patterns and focus on your strenths and virtues. Show appreciation, love and acceptance to the ones around you, so you too can experience the same.

Decide which parts of your personality you would like to Strengthen and which portions you would like to let go. Release the negative portions of your personality which no longer serve you in a beneficial manner. Let go any negative beliefs you have that have held you back.

Start to absorb new feelings of happiness and the expectancy of great things to happen. Stay in a positive and motivated attitude, to attract in more positive experiences to your life. Your attitude will always be is the key factor in your own success.

"The greatest discovery of all time is that a person can change his future by merely changing his attitude."

—Oprah Winfrey

BAD BYTCH RULE NO. 65: If you are unhappy about something in your life, I can guarantee you are spending your time or your money in the wrong places.

"Most people are about as happy as they chose to be."

—Abraham Lincoln

Organization is the first rule in heaven. Take a very good look at your day and where you are spending your time. Anything that is taking up your time, but is not benefiting your life needs to be traded in for more positive behaviors.

Reduce clutter in your home so positive energy can flow freely through. Organize your all your important paper work. Cut back on over communication with negative influences. Create balance in your life between work and personal time.

Make sure every single cent that you earn is carefully accounted for. Watch your money like a hawk to ensure it is being spent in the right places. Never waste your time nor money on experiences that do not serve you in the most empowering ways.

Make good things come true for yourself through your own actions. Make your work invigorating and inspiring.

"Out of clutter, find simplicity. From discord, find harmony. In the middle of difficulty lies opportunity. " – Albert Einstein

BAD BYTCH RULE NO. 66: GET ACTIVE! When you become active and take the first step, the next step will reveal itself.

"Faith is taking the first step even when you don't see the whole staircase."

-Dr. Martin Luther King Jr

Once you have set your core foundation and created goals, it is time to put your plan into action. Take the very first step in faith and know once you have made it through the first step, the second step will be shown and so on and so forth. Gladly put forth the needed every day to achieve your goals.

"Things may come to those who wait, but only the things left by those who hustle."

- Abraham Lincoln

BAD BYTCH RULE NO. 67: Avoid stupid disputes. When you spend time arguing with an idiot, people peering in from a distance cannot tell who is who.

"When arguing with a fool, don't answer their foolish arguments, or you become as foolish as they are."

– Proverbs 26:4

Nothing will ever be solved through an argument. This rule applies for arguing in person, over the phone, via email or the worst yet, through social networks.

Watching an argument take place is like watching a train wreck. It is hard to look away from and hard not to take sides. Most people don't get to see all the circumstances that led up to the outbursts, they just get to see the outburst. You will be tried in the court of public opinion based simply on the dispute, not the conditions leading up to it. Do yourself a favor and always take the high road.

You can chose for every experience you encounter in life to be positive, purposeful and meaningful. Avoid negative disputes like the plague. Find more practical ways to deal life's disagreements or simply agree to disagree.

"Anger is never without an argument, but seldom with a good one."

– Indira Gandhi

BAD BYTCH RULE NO. 68: In order to get ahead in life, every single day you have to do something to make your tomorrow better.

"Education is the passport to the future, for tomorrow belongs to those who prepare for it today."

— Malcolm X

Every day you encounter in life is an opportunity to take action to bring you closer your dreams. Make sure that each day you make choices that will make your tomorrow easier. This can be as small as laying out your clothing the night before for the next day, packing your lunch the night before, or making sure there is gas in your car the night before. Be your own best friend. Leave yourself little boosts and pick me ups that will make your day more smoothly.

Have a list of achievements that you want to make every single day. Try not to leave tasks undone today for you to have to complete tomorrow. Know which tasks take up more time and energy. Those are the ones you need to tackle first to make sure they get done.

The most important thing to do is to keep moving ahead forward. Invest in a nice sports watch so you can keep track of your time easier. Invest in a good calendar to keep track of your appointments and deadlines. The effort that you put in today is what creates your tomorrow. To create love and happiness in your life, ensure all of your actions are positive and helpful. Be mindful of your thoughts, your emotions and your attitudes. They will also help create your future.

An absolute sound investment you can make in your future is education. A degree is an accomplishment that you can always take with you. Invest in making your future visions come true with solid choices today.

"Vision without execution is a hallucination."

— Thomas A. Edison

BAD BYTCH RULE NO. 69: Fair exchange is not a robbery. If a situation is mutually benefitting it may be worth partaking in.

"Whatever the mind of man can conceive and believe, it can achieve. Thoughts are things! And powerful things at that, when mixed with definiteness of purpose, and burning desire, can be translated into riches."

— Napoleon Hill

You can accomplish anything when you set your mind to do it. You can accomplish a whole lot more when you team up with people whom are already motivated with the same desires and worth ethics as you. Believe in your ability to form valuable partnerships with other success driven individuals.

Bartering can be a powerful tool in a business environment. Trade your professional services for someone else's products or services that you find useful. **Establish a networking agreement which is mutually benefitting to both parties involved.**

Create clear concise referral programs within your own professional network. Make sure that each party involved has their own specialty that they handle and it doesn't step on the toes of anyone else within the network. Consider splitting advertisement and promotional costs.

Exercise your professional network to the fullest. There is power in numbers and in joint efforts. Be willing to cooperate and learn from each other. The goal is to achieve a long lasting prosperous business relationship.

"Coming together is a beginning.

Keeping together is progress.

Working together is success."

  - Henry Ford

BAD BYTCH RULE NO. 70: Attempting to comprehend the actions of a crazy person, could make yourself go crazy! Keep your sanity and walk away.

"The statistics on sanity are that one out of every four Americans is suffering from some form of mental illness. Think of your three best friends. If they're okay, then it's you." —Rita Mae Brown

At some point along the way, you will encounter people whose actions in life do not make sense to you. You may wonder why they make the choices they do. You may witness them let valuable opportunities slip away from them. To truly understand someone else's reasoning, you have to be able to put your foot in their shoe and experience everything that they have experienced.

My fellow Bad Bytchez, before you are so quick to try and understand the method behind their madness, pause for a moment. What if this person is demented? If this person is mentally unstable, putting your foot in their shoe may not be the best idea for you. Learn how to accept someone else's life choices. Even if they do not make sense to you, still respect them. Don't drive yourself crazy trying to understand or reason with them. Accept them for who they are and keep it moving.

"Insanity: doing the same thing over and over again and expecting different results."
— Albert Einstein

BAD BYTCH RULE NO. 71: When unsure when making a business decision, ask yourself what would Oprah do. I call this the O Factor.

"My philosophy is that not only are you responsible for your life but doing the best at this moment puts you in the best place for the next moment."

– Oprah Winfrey

Let me give you a quick breakdown of Oprah's yearly earnings. She makes $315,000,000 a year, $26,000,000 per month, $6,000,000 per week, $35,000 an hour, $600 a minute and $10 a second. She is a living legend in our day. Not only is she financially wealthy, she is also spiritually wealthy.

Follow her work. Oprah teaches that energy is the very essence of life and the importance of maintaining positive energy levels every day. Anything done with the intent of helping someone brings positive energy. Everything in life that you encounter can be meaningful and purposeful.

Set a goal for yourself and know what it takes to reach that goal. Maintain your focus and take opportunities as they are given to you. Know that if you work hard every day and focus, you too can reach the same levels that Oprah has. Oprah has never told anyone of us that it was easy, but she did tell us if we work hard we can achieve anything that we set out to.

When you are feeling frustrated or questioning a business or personal matter, take a few moments to research some of Oprah's teachings. Also, look in to the other great teachers that she has referred us to over the years. I promise you, they will help you to transform your life in the very best way possible.

"I don't think of myself as a poor deprived ghetto girl who made good. I think of myself as somebody who from an early age knew I was responsible for myself, and I had to make good."

—Oprah Winfrey

BAD BYTCH RULE NO. 72: If someone is talking shyt about you, but they make less money than you, then they are jealous. If someone is talking shyt about you and they make more money than you then they are scared.

"If I wasn't winning, you wouldn't care."

—Nicki Minaj

For someone to have the power to hurt you or cut you down, you have to give it to them. Just as easily as you can chose to give in to their malicious ways, you can chose not to.

Look into the nucleus of the negativity. If someone is going out there way to talk shyt about you, but they have not even reached your level yet, spiritually or financially then they are jealous. Flat out jealously.

Bad Bytchez gladly take constructive criticism from someone whom is a master in the field that I am working in, or from someone whom is more spiritually advanced than me. Other than that let their criticisms go in one ear and out the muthafukkin other.

Now on the flip side, if someone is talking shyt about you and they have already achieved a higher level of success than you, than they are very afraid of you. They are afraid that you are coming for their spot. They are afraid that you will even surpass them. Let their shyt talking motivate you and fuel your flame even more to succeed even more.

"Haters: they hate what you look like, whacha wearing, whacha drivin, whacha think about, whacha talk about...they fuckin hate it but you gonna have to understand that's the way it is........Have you eva caught a muthafuka starin at you with the I just caught the stomach virus face? You ever just out yo peripheral like...like everything about you just fuck with them."

   – Katt Williams

BAD BYTCH RULE NO. 73: Aggressively pursue your goals and dreams in life or you will end up working for someone whom did.

"If ya'll can't already see I aint worried about ya'll cause I'm already me."

— Jay Z

You have to be an active and aggressive participant in pursuing your own dreams. It is easy to get caught up in the monotony of everyday life. Just maintaining your current lifestyle is hard these days. If you focus all your energy on just maintaining, next thing you know, you look up and be left behind.

Your classmates or colleagues may not be so willing to confiscate their dreams. They won't slow down their progress to wait for yours. By the time you get focused and motivated, they will have already surpassed you.

Stay on top of your game at all times. Keep your focus by writing out your long term goals and short term goals. Adjust and track your progress daily to make these goals come true.

Don't waste your time worrying about what the next person is doing. This would take your concentration off of what you're doing. Make sure that you give your dreams 110% of your attention every day. Live out your today in a way that you won't regret tomorrow.

"Be nice to nerds. Chances are you'll end up working for one."

— Bill Gates

BAD BYTCH RULE NO. 74: Keep your faith when you find yourself going through life's trials and tribulations. Quickly figure out what the lesson you need to learn out of the experience. Learn the lesson quickly and completely then move along.

"When thou passest through the waters, I will be with thee; and through the rivers, they shall not overflow thee: when thou walkest through the fire, thou shalt not be burned." —Isaiah 43:2

Always keep your faith no matter what you are going through. Watch that you do not be overcome by stumbling blocks that are put in your path. The tougher times are put there to teach you valuable lessons. Instead of letting yourself react negatively, look for the essence of goodness which could come out of the situation. Look for the rainbows when the sky is overcast.

Figure out what the Universe is trying to teach you. What can you change to make sure that you never encounter the some problems again. Appreciate the lesson and quickly move along past it. Get back on your path and proceed full-steam ahead!

"And this, our life, exempt from public haunt, finds tongues in trees, books in the running brooks, sermons in stones, and good in everything."
– William Shakespeare

BAD BYTCH RULE NO. 75: Procrastination is the serial killer of goals and dreams. Bad Bytchez do not use any excuses, get it done today!

"Peace I leave with you my peace I give unto you: not as the world giveth, give I unto you. Let not your heart be troubled, neither let it be afraid." –

– John 14:1, 27

Procrastination is putting off essential tasks to another time or date. Procrastination is a product of fear. Fear of how powerful you truly are. Fear of what you can accomplish when you go full throttle towards it. Procrastination is fueled by self-doubt. It is present due to the lack of motivation to get up and get shyt done.

If you find yourself making one sorry a$$ excuse, after sorry a$$ excuse, then you are procrastinating. Another form of procrastination is when you chose to busy yourself doing small less important tasks, rather than accomplishing big defeats. **Instead of looking for excuses not to do it, find reasons why you should get it done as soon as possible.**

Imagine your life if every single day you went in as hard as you could. Imagine a strict set regimen where you go to bed at a certain time, wake up at a certain time, and calculate every moment of your day making sure that you are using your time as beneficial as humanely possible. Now that would be an ideal day indeed.

Now, go back through that scenario and be a littler nicer to yourself. Schedule in yourself a few breaks and periods of down time that you have designated for rest or enjoyment. Once you have that schedule mastered, switch your goal to be more proficient. Tackle the harder tasks immediately. Work very hard and quickly, so you become so proficient that you have all your business handled by a certain time every day. After you have achieved a large amount for one day, you spend the rest of the day for your personal enjoyment. **Most winners try to achieve at least three large goals per day. A Bad Bytch is capable of achieving way more than that.**

"Never put off till tomorrow what you can do today."

- Thomas Jefferson

BAD BYTCH RULE NO. 76: **A persons inability to handle your success is simply their problem and not yours. Stay focused and stay on your path.**

"It doesn't matter if a million people tell you what you can't do, or if ten million tell you no. If you get one yes from God that's all you need."
— Tyler Perry

The only person that has to believe in your vision for it to come true is you. Everyone else can discourage you. Everyone else can envy you. **Block it all negativity and believe in the power you have within yourself to make your dreams come true.** Go inside yourself and visit God. Ask that He blesses your vision. Ask for His approval only. Ask that he blesses your journey. So all mistakes made along the way will not be vain. You will learn and grow from them. You will survive them.

As you become successful, there will be people with in your inner circle that will take joy in your success and congratulate you. Then there will be a few in your life which cannot handle your success. They may approach you with cautionary tales. Some may want to attribute your success to factors other than your hard work. Survive their attacks on you.

Stay Strong my fellow Bad Bytchez. There is no harm in their envy. This is just God's way to make sure that we are secure in ourselves. **If someone is unable to handle your success, that is their problem and not yours. Pray for them and continue being successful!**

"You make mistakes, but I don't have any regrets. I'm the kind of person who takes responsibility for it and deals with it. I learn from everything I do. I work very hard, I have so many things going on in my life. Get to know me and see who I am."

- Kim Kardashian

BAD BYTCH RULE NO. 77: Emotions have absolutely no place in Business. When you are at work, check all that bullshyt in at the door. Emotions will cloud your judgment.

"I don't display emotions. I have every feeling that everyone else has but I've developed ways to suppress them. Anger is one of my most comfortable feelings."

— 50 Cents

During your business day, it is imperative that you are able to think clearly. Bad Bytch's make business decisions based off their intelligence, never based of their emotions. When you are at home getting ready to head into work, make sure you put your big girl panties on. Check all your personal bullshyt in at the door. Emotions do not belong in your office space.

Become a different person at work. Become someone whose focus is to simply get your job done and get it done well. Switch it to straight Beast Mode. Know that you have the strength inside of you to achieve and conquer. Carefully let your colleagues only see positive emotions come from you. Be professional in the workplace. Simply turn off any negative feelings. Your negative feelings could cloud your judgment on important business matters. The most dangerous of all negative emotions to bring into the work place is anger. Anger can quickly spread to others if it is not quickly self-contained. That's the shyt that will get you fired or make it so no one wants to work with you.

Switch your inner frequency to a good energy vibe. Have unwavering faith that there is enough strength in you to make it successfully through this day and every day. Feel prosperous! When you are at work, it is essential that people judge you off the quality of your work, not off your emotional outbursts, your personal life, or your erratic behavior. You want your co-workers to be able to depend on you. They should be confident in your work and your ability to do a good job.

"I'm aware if I'm playing at my best I'm tough to beat. And I enjoy that."

– Tiger Woods

BAD BYTCH RULE NO. 78: To achieve what you have never achieved before, you have to step out of your comfort zone and do things you have never done before.

"I am a walking piece of art every day, with my dreams and my ambitions forward at all times in an effort to inspire my fans to lead their life in that way."

— Lady GaGa

Learn to be bold! **Step outside what your normal life is and live your ideal life.** Decide exactly how you want to live. We don't have to act accordingly to what society tells us is right. We don't have to dress accordingly to what society tells us is appropriate. **We can make our own damn rules and make society deal with that.**

Be yourself and make others accept you for it. Society is extremely critical. You could be Mother Theresa and people will still judge you and criticize you for it. You might as well be yourself and make society accept you.

People may not understand you, your dreams and your own personal style. Still don't change it for them, continue being yourself. To conform is to sacrifice your creativity. Keep your personal individuality. It may hurt not to be accepted everywhere by everyone at first, but you are opening up doors for everyone to love and accept themselves to be who they are. Artist cannot fear to make art. Make your own way just as you are.

The majority of the world's most talented people are considered to be eccentric by society's standards. However their fan base is still strong. They are still making money and they still have appreciation for their art. Leave your comfort zone. Reach inside to bring out your higher self and create your own masterpieces.

"But for me to have the opportunity to stand in front of a bunch of executives and present myself, I had to hustle in my own way. I can't tell you how frustrating it was that they didn't get that. No joke – I'd leave meetings crying all the time."

– Kanye West

BAD BYTCH RULE NO. 79: To simply wish for something to change is not enough, you absolutely have to will it to happen! If you want to see Change in your life, GET ACTIVE TODAY!

"Change will not come if we wait for some other person or some other time. We are the ones we've been waiting for. We are the change that we seek."
—President Barack Obama

The moment that you decide that you want something different for your life, you must be willing to assume full responsibility in making it different. To wish is simply not enough. We are no longer riding tricycles. Our training wheels are off and it is full grown woman status time. Once you decide a strong, positive change is appropriate, also decide how you are going to accomplish it.

Do not make any excuse, do not procrastinate. Get busy today. It is time to lace up your boot straps and start working towards a new and better you.

"Be miserable. Or motivate yourself. Whatever has to be done, it's always your choice."
— Wayne Dyer

BAD BYTCH RULE NO. 80: Never lie or use deception in attempts your to get ahead in life. Lies are destructive and warp the mind and physical body. Truth is like fertilizer it promotes growth and is eternal.

"I come to the world to bear witness to truth. Everyone who belongs to the truth listens to my voice." – Jesus

Every day you must behave in a way that acknowledges that what you do and say to others will inevitable come back to you. This is karma and this is very real. Your karma can be very good or you can accumulate negative karma which you will have to answer to.

Evil is DISHONESTY. Deception is a fundamental trait of Evil people. Always be honest with yourselves and others. Always let people know up front what they are dealing with and allow them to choose if they want to partake in it. One lie, leads to another lie, leads to another lie until you are finally tangled up in a web of your own deceit.

Learn to be always be honest with yourself. Acknowledge people and situations for how they truly are. Acknowledge your true feelings towards people and situations. Treat people according to the truth. React according to the truth. Truth is like fertilizer for growth. Truth is eternal and lives forever. Anything born of falsehoods is destined to parish. Never get caught up in imagined circumstances.

"False words are not only evil in themselves, but they infect the soul with evil." – Socrates

BAD BYTCH RULE NO. 81: Reward yourself for a job well done!
You have every right to be proud of your accomplishments!

"The fact of the matter is, you don't give up what's natural. Anything I've fantasized about, I've done."

– Ray Charles

You did that!!!! Be so proud of you!! A Bad Bytch is a piece of work indeed. Every time you talk to us, we are gonna be telling you about a magazine cover we just hit. We are gonna be celebrating a major deal we just landed. "Hey, did you check your mail??? Did you get your invite to our graduation??!!?" Hell Yeah!! You are going to be hearing about our accomplishments constantly because we work hard for them.

Allow every good feeling and rush of excitement to go through you. Take that momentum and go even hard achieving. Turn it in to a string of wins for you. Stay humble, but stay confident also. When your work hard to achieve something you have every right to be cocky as a muthafukka for a moment. Hang your diploma up high. Put it right next to your other one. We deserve it ladies!

Make sure you keep track of all your accomplishments and the dates you achieved them. That way it you can easily update your resume. You do have a resume, don't you? Stay on top your business ladies.

Also, look out for patterns in the numbers. Did they date that you graduate happen to be your Grandmothers Birthday? Was the time you got that important phone call, the same time as your moment of birth? Look for these happy coincidences God sends us to remind us we are on the right track.

Celebrate all your accomplishments. Give yourself little rewards. For example, if you make your weight loss goal, buy yourself a new outfit. Book yourself a massage after a long days work. Have a night out with your girls for getting your big raise! Throw yourself the biggest graduation barbeque ever. Constantly treat yourself to something that will keep you happy and motivated throughout your journey to success.

"Your on your way. Keep going, and delight in the wonderful rewards you've already started to create for yourself."

— Ralph Marston

BAD BYTCH RULE NO. 82: Never allow your goals or dreams to become watered down by other people's opinions on what you "should" do.

" I heard motherfuckers saying they made Hov...Made Hove say, Ok so, make another Hov"

– Jay Z

Everyone and they muthafukkin momma will have an opinion on what you should do with your career and how you should live your life. If you take the time to listen to their opinions, your own personal brand may become watered down. When you are in need of advice, the best place to go is within yourself.

Go someplace peaceful and solitude. Relax your mind and release all worries and anxiety. Meditate on the questions you have, then quiet your mind and listen for answers.

These answers may come in visions or inspired thoughts, but they will be true to you and your higher self. Implement your visions to achieve success. Focus on your prosperity and ignore any negative people or negative emotions.

"Don't Change So People Will Like You. Be Yourself So The Right People Will Love The Real You......."

– Q Founder of World Star

BAD BYTCH RULE NO. 83: Show yourself approved unto God! Let everyone else fall to the side. When you have God's approval, no one else's even matters.

"Ask God to show you what you need to change. Accept others for who they are and see how God works in you to complete your joy." — Rihanna

Let go of anyone else's opinion. Let go of anyone else's judgments. **Only God can judge you. It was written.** Go directly to the source of all things good. Run all your life choices through God first. Make choices that you know **He** would be proud of you for.

In no manner does this mean you have to be a goody two shoes. You could be a certified bad girl, but still Love your Maker and make Him proud of You! Only man looks upon things of the day, God looks at your intent. Are your intentions good or are your intentions bad? When you do all things with good intent, God will support you. When you have God's support who can really be against you?

"But seek ye first the kingdom of God, and his righteousness; and all these things shall be added unto you." —Matthew 6:33

BAD BYTCH RULE NO. 84: Utilize the Power of Attraction to get what you want. Appreciate and make the best of what you do have on a regular basis and it will attract more. Always show gratitude for all your blessings, family and close friends to attract more blessings and more love.

"Whatever relationships you have attracted in your life at this moment, are precisely the ones you need in your life at this moment. There is a hidden meaning behind all events, and this hidden meaning is serving your own evolution."
— Deepak Chopra

You attract certain people and certain situations into your life through your thoughts and your attitude. When you have this information being given to you through all the great spiritual teachers in history, why not use it to your advantage?

If you walk around here with a negative a$$ attitude, always complaining and shyt, you will attract to yourself more shyt to complain about. Do you want to have more to complain about? If the answer is no, then learn to shut the fukk up and appreciate what you do have.

Thank God for all your blessings and count them on the regular. **Having an attitude that is always grateful and always loving will attract more things to love and be grateful for.** Make the absolute best out of what you do have in hand every single day.

Respond to everything with compassion and kindness, so you may experience them in your life.

"Successful people make money. It's not that people who make money become successful, but that successful people attract money. They bring success to what they do."

– Wayne Dyer

BAD BYTCH RULE NO. 85: Never be afraid to stand your ground, even if it means you have to stand there alone. Always BELIEVE in Yourself! Always Think for Yourself! Even if your opinion is different than the vast majority of your peers, stand up for what you believe in!

"Courage is the most important of all the virtues, because without courage you can't practice any other virtue consistently. You can practice any virtue erratically, but nothing consistently without courage."

-Maya Angelou

You chose your cause in life. You chose your mission. You chose your career. Choose your own morals. Choose who and what you believe in. These are the choices you made because it is what best represented you and what you believe in. Now, it's up to you to stand by those choices. Sometimes you will have an overwhelming amount of supporters. That is a true blessing and will make your journey a lot easier.

Be prepared to face opposition to your beliefs. Not everyone will be a fan. You will get critiqued. Your choices will be questioned. This is where you have to be courageous and stand your ground.

Even if your beliefs differ from the majority of those around you, stand your ground. Fight for what you believe in. Know that your path is righteous, even if others do not know the same way. Stay strong to your morals. Stay on your grind.

Create your own decisions in life and stick by them. Think for yourself at all times. You are in complete control of the outcome.

"He is a man of courage who does not run away, but remains at his post and fights against the enemy."

–Socrates

BAD BYTCH RULE NO. 86: Visualization is a powerful tool. Put up a picture of your goal and look at it every single day until you achieve it. Seek out life teachers that will help your vision to come true.

"It was all a dream, I used to read Word Up magazine. Salt'n'Pepa and Heavy D up in the limousine. Hangin' pictures on my wall. Every Saturday Rap Attack, Mr. Magic, Marley Marl, I let my tape rock 'til my tape popped."
— *Biggie Smalls*

This is the fun part. This is when you get to decide exactly who you want to be and what you want in life. **To visualize, is to become so clear on what you want in life, that you can picture it vividly.** You are able to recognize it when you see it in magazines.

Try putting up a picture of your goal on your wall. Look at it every single day until you achieve it. **Let that picture remind you that every day you have to work towards your goal in order to make it a reality. Seek out mentors and teachers who can lead you on your path and help make your vision a reality**.

"I've been blessed to find people who are smarter than I am, and they help me to execute the vision I have."
— *Russell Simmons*

BAD BYTCH RULE NO. 87: Don't be afraid to say "No." Some opportunities presented to you are a "Thanks, but No Thanks". Weigh out your options and figure out what is best for you.

"I didn't want to say "No" because I didn't want people to think I'm not nice. And that, to me, has been the greatest lesson of my life: to recognize that I am solely responsible for it, and not trying to please other people, and not living my life to please other people, but doing what my heart says all the time." – Oprah Winfrey

When it comes to business, fukk being nice. Never feel obligated to take on extra work that you do not feel up to. If your heart is not in it, don't do it. Carefully decide what is going to be beneficial to you. **Only enter in to situations that you feel like you can benefit from**. Whether you benefit financially or developmental wise, make sure you benefit.

Some offers will be actually decent offers, but just not good for your career right now. Make sure you turn those away gently. Keep open to the possibility of working together in the future.

If someone makes a business offers to you that is so idiotic that it is offensive, let them know about it. Let them know that you do not work operate yourself or your business like that. A Bad Bytch may have to end up using the "kiss my ass clause". That's when you tell someone "Hell no, I'm not doing that and you can kiss my a$$". Feel free to exercise this right to use the "kiss my a$$ clause" as needed throughout your career.

It is inevitable that in business people will try to get over on you. It is your duty as a Bad Bytch to never allow that to happen. Be hungry, but be picky. Never allow yourself to appear that desperate that you will jump on anything that comes your way. Desperate is not a good look on anyone. Have professional standards for yourself. You simply cannot do business with everyone because everyone's business ethics just aren't there yet.

"Those whom stand for nothing, fall for anything."

— Alexander Hamilton

BAD BYTCH RULE NO. 88: If you see any portion of your life or your behavior spiraling out of control, you MUST immediately take action.

"I'm always trying to do the impossible to please people. It comes from not being secure in myself and not looking at the things within that I have to fix. Sometimes you keep going because you don't want to face the truth."

— Naomi Campbell

The human body with all its beauty and wonder, yet and still no one is perfect. We all make mistakes. We all are a product of our environment. We are a product of what we have been taught to believe what is acceptable and unacceptable. We are influenced by our family and our peers. Not always is the influence we receive positive. **When you find yourself engaging in addictive or negative behavior, be intelligent enough to acknowledge it and courageous enough to take action.**

If your loved ones are coming to you concerned about your behavior or bad habits, don't immediately blow them off. Take a moment to step outside yourself and consider what they are saying. It takes a very strong person to look at themselves from an outsider's point of view. Acknowledge any behavior that is damaging to your health or your spiritual growth. Do not try to make up excuses for it. Don't give any justifications. Just acknowledge the behavior and the need to begin the healing process.

Remember to love and respect yourselves at all times. There is no shame in admitting when you need help. Seek out support, counseling or medical attention if needed.

It is through our mistakes in life that we learn our greatest lessons. Do not be ashamed that you went down the wrong path. Instead, hold your high and start making moves to get yourself back on the right path.

"The greatest glory in living lies not in never falling, but in rising every time we fall."

— Nelson Mandela

BAD BYTCH RULE NO. 89: You should never feel "trapped" at a particular place or in a particular situation. Keep a safety net and an escape plan ready.

"An artist must be free to choose what he does, certainly, but he must also never be afraid to do what he might choose."
– Langston Hughes

For years of my life, I felt trapped at a job I held. I felt trapped there because I knew it was a good job. I knew the pay was exceptional. The benefits were good. I knew as long as I worked there my family was taken care of. However the job was surrounded with negativity. I got to the point where I did not enjoy this job anymore. I dreaded going to work there, but I felt trapped in the situation.

I began repeatedly hearing an angelic voice telling me that it was time to move on to pursue my dreams. Yet I was still fearful of the unknown. I kept going to work long hours and feeling trapped. I still kept hearing the angelic voice encouraging me to move on past the job more often and more loudly. I had visions of what I should be doing. I was able to chart out plans and time lines from them. I began randomly meeting important people in the field I wanted to be in. I found networking with them to be very encouraging and motivating. I finally made a choice to start actually pursuing a different career.

I began reading books. I read a lot of books about spiritual development. I read a lot of books about the greatest artist, philosophers and musicians that had ever lived. I looked at the biggest names today in the entertainment industry and what their life experiences were like on the road to success. I kept seeing a reoccurring theme throughout all their lives. **The Greatest Legends in History have Great Faith! They had faith in themselves, but most importantly they had faith in God. No matter which religion they were, no matter what name they called God by, they had unwavering faith in this higher power.** It is through that faith, you will learn to believe in the powers you have inside of you to be an heir to the throne.

Believe in the Promises that He has made to you. Start expecting great things for yourself. Start looking at the clues and encouragement that history's greatest teachers is left behind for us. Look at the work of the current heroes and she-roes we have in our generation. All of them are at where they are at because they let go of their fears and actively pursued their dreams.

My fellow Bad Bytchez, just as I had to learn myself, you must let go of any and all fear. **LET GO OF FEAR AND KEEP YOUR FAITH!** Fear will keep you trapped in mediocre lifestyles and in unhappy careers. Live with a purpose that is more than just maintaining a decent lifestyle. . Live with a purpose that is higher than yourself. Live with a sincere intense passion. Learn to make money doing something that you truly love. Believe in your power to be successful at doing what your love. Don't let another moment go by without claiming your throne as a rightful heir to His Kingdom.

"the number one cause of failure in this country is the fear of failure" — Steve Harvey

BAD BYTCH RULE NO. 90: Be very aware of your energy. Accept only Positive Energy from others. Don't allow them to trap you with negative outlooks.

"Whenever I feel bad, I use the feeling to motivate me to work harder. I only allow myself one day to feel sorry for myself." — Beyoncé

Even in your darkest moments of despairs, be able to look around you and find things that you can celebrate and thank the Lord for. Your emotions are a key to what your energy is. When you feel anger, sadness or disappointment your mind is transmitting out negative energy from you. The energy you put out is what you will attract back to you. **Limit your time that you spend complaining or feeling sorry for yourself.**

Identify sources that consistently bring negativity in to your life. Do you have a friend whom always just seems to get caught up in unnecessary drama? They call you 3 million damn times with bad news after bad news. **Drama queens will take you off focus and disturb your life with their bullshyt. Cut them.**

Another female that a Bad Bytch needs to be on the lookout for is one whom has insecurities that they attempt to deflect on you. They will attempt to "caution you" from following your dreams because of their fears. **Keep in mind that those are their fears and not yours.** Stay on the Positive Path and let them hoes miss you with their bullshyt.

Learn how to change your energy channel to a positive one. Feel happy, grateful and joyful so you attract more positive experiences to your life. Make it your business to find hobbies that you enjoy. Have special locations you like to go because it makes you happy. Have special people you can go to that bring joy and motivation into your life. Ignore the drama queens and the worry-warts. **Spend the majority of the time surrounding yourself by positive, confident, like-minded people.**

"To be blessed and not to celebrate is prideful and arrogant in my book. Give God praise. You've sure complained enough."
—Reverend Run

BAD BYTCH RULE NO. 91: **Misery loves company! Don't get to caught up in other peoples sob stories. Woe is me never solves shyt.**

"You messed up my self-esteem....Bitch it's called SELF ESTEEM! It's the esteem of ya Mutha Fuckin Self Bitch......How did I fuck up how YOU feel about YOU?"
— Katt Williams

Miserable people are sneaky as fuck. They will come into your life just to try to bring you down to their level. They will attempt to confuse you into believing that their well-being is in your hands rather than their own. Hell naw, they don't want to take responsibilities for their choices that made them miserable. Admitting they had a problem would be them making the first step in healing the problem. What would they want to heal for, then they wouldn't have your attention and sympathy. They may try to get you to heal all their problems for them. Somehow, they will make their personal problems your fault.

A Bad Bytch can see through the miserable bullshyt from a mile away. If you sit back and listen to too many woe is me stories, you may accidentally start telling a few yourself. Know the difference between a good person going through of tough time and a miserable person suffering through repeated poor life choices. Avoid them miserable muthafukkas. They will tell you their heart wrenching stories to attempt to take you up outta your true character and spark negative emotions.

Stay focused, so that you will not be brought down to their level. Deflect their negativity and sob stories. Someone whom cannot see the love and blessings within their own life, will certainly not want you to see you it in yours either.

"I don't have to go around trying to save everybody anymore; that's not my job."

—Jada Pinkett Smith

BAD BYTCH RULE NO. 92: Time machines do not exist. Instead of obsessing over your past, start to obsess over your future and all the endless possibilities you have.

"Every time you are tempted to react in the same old way, ask if you want to be a prisoner of the past or a pioneer of the future"

— Deepak Chopra

Bad Bytch's are not victims. **We are products of our past, but we do not have to keep being victims of it. Release yourself from negative memories and negative feelings. Stop re-living traumatic situations. Address them. Learn from them. Then grow past them.** Never make choices that will force you back into the same negative predicament. That is not growth. That is descending. Bad Bytchez don't descend. We **ASCEND**! Always keep your muthafukkin head up and faced towards your future.

Make a choice today to no longer be a victim of past situations. Learn to let go. Let go of fears and old hurts. **Release absolutely anything in your past that has been holding you back. One negative moment in your life does not determine the theme of your entire journey.** Understand the bigger picture of your lifetime journey. **Learn how to accept the world as it is. You will inevitable face situations that are good and bad.** Trust in your ability to create joy and happiness in your life. Learn to trust in God that you will never be faced with anything that you cannot make it through.

Acknowledge your hurt, and then allow yourself to heal. Know that your purpose here is much bigger than a few bad experiences. Know that your soul has grown and developed. Know that you have furthered your evolution. Then, let go! Let go of negative thought patterns, so you can embrace new feelings of peace and confidence.

Absorb all positive new feelings with love. Continue on your ultimate journey with a big heart and a lot of compassion towards others that may be going through tough times. Give and receive love easily. The more love and compassion that you create for others, the more you will experience in your life time.

"Yesterday's dead, Tomorrow's unborn,

So there's nothing to fear And nothing to mourn

For all that is past And all that has been

Can never return To be lived once again"

— Helen Steiner Rice

BAD BYTCH RULE NO. 93: Cultivate the ability to laugh. Never lose your sense of humor when dealing with everyday bullshyt.

"I always want to know what's wrong with you, why you ain't smiling. That's just my character; I just love people and want to see people having a good time."
– Wyclef Jean

Prior to being born, you were somewhere in heaven writing out your life plan with the Good Lord. In that life plan, you chose to write in silly little inconveniences for yourself.. The inconvenience may be short lived, but it will be enough to slow down your day and distract you for a bit. This will help you to become light-hearted. It will teach you to remain focused despite what is going on around.

Never lose your sense of humor when dealing with everyday bullshyt. Be able to see the ridiculousness in it all. Some days may be so frustrating, that you have to laugh to keep from going crazy. Laugh to keep from crying. Don't let lives little hiccups like a flat tire or parking ticket ruin your day. Keep everything on a positive level and smile. Slow down for a moment, correct the issue and keep going.

Do not become so easily offended. Keep your sense of humor in all situations.

"I love those who can smile in trouble, who can gather strength from distress, and grow brave by reflection. 'Tis the business of little minds to shrink, but they whose heart is firm, and whose conscience approves their conduct, will pursue their principles unto death."
– Leonardo da Vinci

BAD BYTCH RULE NO. 94: Learn to Give and Receive LOVE!!

"Neither a lofty degree of intelligence nor imagination nor both together go to the making of genius. Love, love, love, that is the soul of genius."
– Wolfgang Amadeus Mozart

Love alone is enough to make your experience here on earth worthwhile. When the world is too loud, **Love** will help you remain calm and well centered. When everything else is taken away from you, the **Love** will remain. When all else is forgotten, the **Love** will be remembered.

The world around us will feel cold and uncertain at times. With Love, you will be able to remain calm and well centered. The **Love** that you give and receive will be enough to uplift you to create joy and happiness in your life. You will attract more wonderful things into your life. You will be able to cope with stress and pressure much easier. When life is coming at you in a fast pace, with love you will still feel happy and relaxed.

Life will still be filled with hurdles and difficult decisions every single day. When you are a Loving person you will be filled with enough courage and confidence to move on forward with your journey. Have a big heart. Laugh and smile often. Let love flow through you easily and naturally.

"People are often unreasonable, irrational, and self-centered. Forgive them anyway.

If you are kind, people may accuse you of selfish, ulterior motives. Be kind anyway.

If you are successful, you will win some unfaithful friends and some genuine enemies. Succeed anyway.

If you are honest and sincere people may deceive you. Be honest and sincere anyway.

What you spend years creating, others could destroy overnight. Create anyway.

If you find serenity and happiness, some may be jealous. Be happy anyway.

The good you do today, will often be forgotten. Do good anyway.

Give the best you have, and it will never be enough. Give your best anyway.

In the final analysis, it is between you and God. It was never between you and them anyway"

 - Mother Teresa

BAD BYTCH RULE NO. 95: Keep your muthafukkin personal life personal.

"I'm not one of those people that goes into details of my personal life on national TV to get attention. Some things are better left unsaid"

– Mariah Carey

This is real-life, not a soap opera. **Never air out your personal relationship, business or family matters in public.** It is inviting criticisms and judgment from the court of public opinion. You are opening yourself up to appear weak and vulnerable. Most muthafukkas who offer you an opinion, don't have an opinion that matters. You will get people talking shyt about you, but not offer to help you.

Everyone needs to vent sometimes, but a social network site is not a place to do it. **Keep your personal tirades about your relationship drama or family drama off of twitter and facebook.** Call a friend to vent, don't go on line begging people for sympathy. Most of the people that see you having a public tirade will judge you or laugh at you. The rest of the people have they on muthafukkin problems to worry about. Invest in a good diary. Don't make a fool out of yourself.

Bad Bytchez do not do twitter beef or facebook drama. It is strange and hopeless to create on-line bullshyt that may end up getting played out in real life. Remember, you have complete control of the image that you display on public networks. **I have diagnosed many people with depression or mental illnesses based off their tweets or facebook status's.** It is truly an awkward moment to find out a colleague or family member is truly a psycho or drama queen on line.

There is something to be said about having a peaceful, drama-free life-style. That is a life-style that your peers can look up to. Everyone experiences drama and bullshyt. People just tend to react with it differently. A Bad Bytch will keep her issues private and find positive ways to overcome them.

"There was a time in my life when I thought I had everything - millions of dollars, mansions, cars, nice clothes, beautiful women, and every other materialistic thing you can imagine. Now I struggle for peace. "

— Richard Pryor

BAD BYTCH RULE NO. 96: Spend less time bragging and boasting about your skills and more time perfecting your craft! Whatever it is that you do, be the absolute best at it.

"Luck has nothing to do with it, because I have spent many, many hours, countless hours, on the court working for my one moment in time, not knowing when it would come."

— Serena Williams

People are quick to brag about their skills but slow to perfect them. Instead of spending time bragging and trying to convince others that you are the absolute best at what you do, try spending that same amount of time perfecting your craft.

Research the legends in your field and let them inspire you to go harder. Make connections with mentors and great teachers. Practice hard and play harder. Fine tune your skills and abilities. Know all the tricks to your trade. Consistently work hard to become a complete master in your profession.

Once you become an expert in your field, your work will speak for itself. You can stay humble and let your work and your supporters do the bragging for you.

"I've missed more than 9000 shots in my career. I've lost almost 300 games. 26 times, I've been trusted to take the game winning shot and missed. I've failed over and over and over again in my life. And that is why I succeed."

-Michael Jordan

BAD BYTCH RULE NO. 97: Always have some place loving and peaceful you can go to quiet your mind. Meditating will help you recharge and get refocused.

'I'm most concerned about is finding inner peace and happiness. All that glitters isn't gold. And there are things better than gold — like having a meaningful conversation, seeing your kids healthy and smiling, and getting along with your mother."

— Sean Diddy Combs

Sometimes this world can be overwhelming. Everywhere you go is just loud and busy. A Bad Bytch needs to have a special secret place they can go to escape from it all. Make it someplace quiet that only you know about that you can go to seek out sanity. It could be a park, a garden or a certain space within your own home. Where ever it is, make sure that you have positive feelings attached the location. That way when you go there, you can absorb all positive energy and recharge.

Another great, helpful secret is meditation. If everyone in the world took 15 minutes a day to meditate, this world we be an amazingly more peaceful, better place. For most people, meditation was just never taught to them. Throughout history, people have coveted information about meditation or ridiculed this practice to ensure others would not live up to their full potential. If you have never tried meditation before, I pray that you do so soon. All lives greatest teachers, leaders and scholars have spent time in solitude to re-charge and re-focus.

Meditation is easy. There are several different styles that you could practice, however for starters I would simply find a place quiet where you can be alone. Quiet your mind. Block out any form of stress or worries. Simply quiet your mind. Next, you listen for answers to your questions and prayers. **If prayer is considered seeking God to ask for guidance, then meditation should be considered listening for God's answers.**

The technology available today has made meditation easier. 97% of Americans own cell phones and there is literally hundreds of apps you can purchase on guided medication. For the full effect, I suggest purchasing a good quality pair of headphones that are sound proofed. That way you can block out any outside noises and listening to the guided meditation app on your phone or computer.

Make Mediation a daily habit for a month and you will see a drastic improvement in your life. You will feel more at peace. You will be more comfortable and confident when making major decisions. Stick with meditating regularly and your life possibilities are endless.

"....when thou prayest, enter into thy closet, and when thou hast shut thy door, pray to thy Father which is in secret; and thy Father which seeth in secret shall reward thee openly." – Matthew 6:6

BAD BYTCH RULE NO. 98: **Never dim your light to allow someone else's light to shine. You have the right to be your absolute best at all times.**

"Let your light so shine before men, that they may see your good works, and glorify your Father which is in heaven." Matthew 5:16

It is your God-given right to be the absolute best you can be at all times. What is it that you are most passionate about? What brings you the most happiness? What area do you have talent in? What are you the best at? **Once you find your niche in life, go for it and go hard!! Let** your light shine!

None of God's children has to hide their talents from the world. They were given to you as your own unique blessing to partake in at will. Fear shall never be on your heart! Proudly take credit for all your hard work. Never let anyone else take credit for what you have done. Believe that you do not have to spend even 5 minutes of your life in someone else's shadow. Ascend to greatness! **Give this world 110% at all times, your life deserves it!!!**

"Our deepest fear is not that we are inadequate. Our deepest fear is that we are powerful beyond measure. It is our light, not our darkness that most frightens us. We ask ourselves, Who am I to be brilliant, gorgeous, talented, fabulous? Actually, who are you *not* to be? You are a child of God. Your playing small does not serve the world. There is nothing enlightened about shrinking so that other people won't feel insecure around you. We are all meant to shine, as children do. We were born to make manifest the glory of God that is within us. It's not just in some of us; it's in everyone. And as we let our own light shine, we unconsciously give other people permission to do the same. As we are liberated from our own fear, our presence automatically liberates others."

—Marianne Williamson

BAD BYTCH RULE NO. 99: Set up a place you call Home. Utilize any symbols, rituals or charms that are special and meaningful to you that you believe will help you along your path.

"For, each soul must come to know its own influence and that which is the most helpful. And if it calls then for self to cleanse the body without and within with pure water, or to fast, or to burn incense, or to set about self certain odors or colors of influences, then—as has been given—use these for thine own development, but be a seeker and a user of that which thou obtainest. For, not only the hearer but rather the doer gains, in its seeking through to the infinite forces and influences. Hence, whether it ids desired from the experience to abstain from this, that or the other influence to obtain the better conditions in self, seek to know these—for thou art not dumb, my brother!"

— Edgar Cayce

You create your own Universe. The powers exists inside you to create the world around you the way you want to live in it. The greatest achievement a Bad Bytch can make in life is to establish a home. **Success always starts within your home.** Unfortunately, today a lot of our younger sisters are not even in a mentality where they can provide stable housing for themselves. It is a Bad Bytch's priority to make sure your basic means of survival are covered. Stable housing is not a want, it is a necessity. I understand you might travel, must but have a home to come home to.

Decorate your home in your favorite everything. Favorite color, favorite fabric, favorite paintings, seriously go wild with it. Set up quiet areas in your house where you can go to peacefully meditate. Bless every corner of your home. Proudly display your accomplishments. Proudly display your children's artwork. Use symbols throughout your home bring that bring you feelings of joy, love and hope. If you like to burn candles, burn candles. If you love incense, burn incense. **Turn your home into a place that an Angel would love to visit.** Often times they do, we just don't know about it.

The symbols or charms that you use in your home you can also find ways to take with you when you travel or have a challenging day ahead. I have known many of people that carried a rock with them that they called the "gratitude rock". It was just a normal rock off the ground somewhere, but every time they looked at the rock it reminded them of all things they were grateful for in their lives.

You can get a little fancier than a rock. For me, I like to carry with me a "Queen" chess piece with me that is carved out of Black & Gray marble. When I look at it throughout the day it reminds me I AM an Heir to the Throne. **Find an item that brings positive, motivating feelings to you that is easy to carry on your person. The strength of this item comes from you.** From the way it makes **you** feel and what it reminds **you** of.

"There is no place like home."

— Dorothy (Wizard of Oz)

BAD BYTCH RULE NO. 100: Share your enlightenment! Share helpful information and encourage other women along the way! Always spread positivity, peace and joy to others so you may know it yourself.

"For every one of us that succeeds, it's because there's somebody was there to show you the way out. The light doesn't always necessarily have to be in your family; for me it was teachers and school."

–Oprah

You are now blessed with knowledge and enlightenment that will help you through life on your path to success. It is now your turn to take the helpful and useful information you have learned and pass it along to others whom may benefit from it. Reach back to our younger generation and help light up the way for a brighter future.

Share information and spread motivation, positivity, peace and joy to the lives of others and it will return to you in the most pure forms. May God Bless all Bad Bytchez that unite to support and encourage one another!

"As we look ahead into the next century, leaders will be those who empower others."

– Bill Gates

Bad Bytch Reading List:

"Employ your time in improving yourself by other men's writings, so that you shall gain easily what others have labored hard for."

—Socrates

The books listed below are a few ones that you will find helpful on your life journey.

1.) *__Holy Bible__* by God

2.) *__A Return To Love: Reflections on the Principles of A Course in Miracles__* by Marianne Williamson

3.) *__The Seven Spiritual Laws of Success__* by Deepak Chopra

4.) *__The Art of War__* by Sun Tzu

5.) *__The 48 Laws of Power__* by Robert Greene

6.) *__The 50th Law__* by 50 Cents

7.) *__A Brief History of Time__* by Stephen Hawking

8.) *__The Secret__* by Rhonda Byrne

9.) *__The Seat of A Soul__* by Gary Zukav and Linda Francis

10.) *__There was a River__* by Thomas Sugrue

11.) *__Think and Grow Rich__* by Napoleon Hill

12.) *__The Law of Attraction__* by Abraham Hicks

LEGION
MUSIC GROUP LLC.

A Personal Note to My Readers
By
Juicey Adoir

To my beautiful ladies that have taken the time to purchase this book and support the Bad Bytch Movement, I Salute you!

I would like to form a Bad Bytch Support Network where us ladies can reach out to one other for love and encouragement throughout our life journeys.

If you found this book helpful or profound in your life, connect with me on Twitter and follow @JuiceyAdoir. Tweet me, I tweet back.

I am interested in your feelings towards The Bad Bytch Rule Book and the power behind it. I am interested in how it touched your life. Tweet me your realizations, your goals or your achievements that you have made.

I will constantly keep posting positive, fun and enlightening information and keep you up to date with our support network.

May God Bless!
Juicey Adoir

Authors Thank You's

First and foremost I attribute all areas of my success to God. All Glory to the Maker of all things Good. I would like to thank my mother Mommy Adoir and my father Douglas and my brothers Christopher and Douglas II.

Much love to my family and crew The Adoir Squadron. Thank you to my sister Cream Adoir for her advice and support over the years, my sister in-law Columbia Adoir for her love and guidance, and my crazy fun loving cousin Kimber Adoir. Special shout out to the Adoir Squadron Modeling Group.

A big thanks to Rikk Reighn whom has been there since day zero, fuck one. Before there was a Juicey, there was a Rikk and before there was either, there was us and we had each other. For me, that would have always been enough. Love forever. Special love and kisses to my three good reasons for everything I do, Salina, Lazarus and Lynx.

Sending thanks and love to my label Legion Music Group. My manager Kiwan R. Lawson. Much love to my annoying lil bro D.J. Hylyte. Kisses to the very talented and next to blow Miss Raindrop. A big thanks to Thomas at Super Model Designs for my beautiful cover and website **www.juiceyadoir.com** ! Thank You to Eric Millionaire for his support. A special thanks to my good friend Aretha Glenn. Thanks to the best Nanny in the whole world, "The New York Nanny" Miss Chavay Williams.

I would like to thank Nicki Minaj for being a motivation for Bad Bytchez everywhere. Thank you to Oprah for showing young black women that they can become any and everything that they desire.

I have a lot of respect for Marcus Blassingame owner of Black Mens Magazine and Urban Ink Magazine. Early on in my modeling career, he taught me that it is up to me to make the difference and take my career to the next level.

Much love and appreciation to DJ Kay Slay owner of Straight Stuntin Magazine for supporting my modeling career from day one, paying for photo shoots and printing me three times. Thank you for the guidance and keeping it real with me.

Thank you to the entire team at World Star. I feel blessed to have connected with Q the founder of World Star very early on in my career and received real boss advice from him about what makes a strong team.

There has been several artist in the industry that took time out their busy career to acknowledge mine. For that I am grateful to Soulja Boy, Waka Flocka, Ace Hood, Big Tigger, Earthquake, Bobby Valentino, Gudda Gudda, 50 Cents, French Montana, and Baby Bash.

I have looked up to the following models throughout my career as a model. I have been blessed to have received love, guidance and support from these amazingly beautiful women: Amber Rose, Rosa Acosta, Lola Monroe, Blac Chyna, Summer Breeze, Wankeago, Haus the Boss, Deelishis, Kat Stacks and Christie Dior.

A special thanks to the team at "The Pretty Girl Rock Show" on IceBreaker Radio including my producer Chosen a.k.a. Charlie and my co-host the amazingly talented Chyna Doll. There are many magazines and websites which have been supportive and helpful during my modeling career and for that I am forever grateful to BossChics.com, Audacity Mag, Bubble Shake Mag, Stunnaz Magazine, Hip Hop Stardum, StarCandie, Naked Hustle and F.E.D.S. Magazine.

For me to have come into the game doing Urban Eye Candy Modeling I have to pay homage to the amazing fact that my support system and fan base has been 85% female. To all my ladies, Bad Bytchez, female bosses, or boss's in training, I do this for YOU! I salute you and commend each and everyone one of you for your efforts and achievements. May God bless you today and every day of your life.

Love Always,

Juicey Adoir